D0672427

NURTURING THE LEADER WITHIN YOUR CHILD

What Every Parent Needs to Know

TIM ELMORE

THOMAS NELSON PUBLISHERS
Nashville

Library of Congress Cataloging-in-Publication Data

Elmore, Tim

      Nurturing the leader within your child : what every parent needs
to know / Tim Elmore.

        p. cm.

     ISBN 0-7852-6614-3

     1. Child rearing. 2. Parenting. 3. Parent and child. 4. Leadership in children.
I. Title.

HQ769 .E5646 2001

649'.1–dc21   2001052181

Dedicated to my two favorite emerging leaders:
Bethany and Jonathan

CONTENTS

FOREWORD

When my good friend and colleague Tim Elmore asked me to write the foreword to this book, I began reflecting on our relationship, and I was startled to realize that I have known Tim for almost two decades. From the moment that I first met Tim, I knew he was special. As a new staff pastor not long out of school himself, he ran the ministry for college students at the church I led, and he was highly effective and influential. There was a reason for that. Tim has many good qualities: he is a tenacious learner; he is a wonderful communicator; and he is the best colleague I've ever had when it comes to teaching from the Bible. But his greatest strength even back then was that he believed that he could change the world. He still believes it, and his work with EQUIP on dozens of college campuses and in countries around the globe bears that out.

Tim's desire to change the world is what prompted him to write *Nurturing the Leader Within Your Child.* He knows that the way to make a better future is to impact the next generation of leaders, to give them a head start in their leadership and help them avoid some difficult pitfalls.

Tim has been passing on leadership teaching to students for almost two decades, and I often think that he now teaches leadership better than I do!

One of my great joys is watching as Tim and his wife, Pam, raise their children. He is doing a wonderful job with them, and of course leadership lessons are a big part of what he does. Next to their relationship with God, leadership is the most important factor in our children's ability to impact the world. Everything rises and falls on that.

There are no guarantees in life. I was very fortunate. I grew up in the home of a great leader, my father, Melvin Maxwell, so I know what kind of impact good leadership development can have on children and their future. I would not be a leader today if it weren't for my parents. However, I also know that in life, almost anything can happen. I have seen good parents with bad kids and bad parents with good kids. But here's the bottom line:

> Our children stand a better chance of developing to their potential if we practice good leadership and teach it to them.

If you want to give your kids the best chance for success, mentor them in leadership, and practice the principles in this book. We may not be able to choose our ancestors, but we can attempt to shape our descendants. If we encourage our children to stand on our shoulders, they will certainly see farther than we have.

John C. Maxwell
Founder, the INJOY Group
2001

INTRODUCTION

YOU AND I—WHO FOR SO LONG WERE KIDS—are now adults. And now we have kids! Perhaps we aren't ready for this. It's scary. Some of us secretly feel like kids who have kids. What is our problem? Why are we uneasy? Do you feel unprepared to be an adequate parent? Like me, do you see potential in your children, but feel you don't have all the resources to help them develop their leadership potential? You may feel a little lost. I have found this scenario to be common across the country. Here's what I hear parents saying:

- I see great gifts inside my child; I just wish I knew how to draw them out.

- I want to be a good parent, but I don't think I'm a good leadership model.

- This generation thinks so differently than the one in which I grew up.

- I'm not sure how to teach leadership to my children.

- I'm so busy I don't know when I'd have time to talk about leadership with my kid.

- My child won't sit through a leadership conference.

- I want my kid to have a head start on life, and work, and career, but . . .

LET ME TELL YOU WHAT I'VE FOUND!

I am not an expert in parenting, and this is not just another parenting book. This book is about developing the leadership potential in your child. I will fill the role of a reporter. Reporters gather information, interview people, investigate, and present information. Reporters don't have all the answers—but they know where to find them.

I am also a practitioner. Each year I have the undeserved privilege of teaching leadership and character values to more than thirty thousand students. Their ages range from five to twenty-four years old, kids from kindergarten to college. They're called the "millennial generation." I love them and have learned a great deal from and about them. Some of this information I'm going to share with you.

In addition, I am also the parent of two millennial generation kids, Bethany and Jonathan. I love them, too. My wife and I long for them to experience everything they need to positively influence their world as they grow up. That's what leadership is—people who influence others in their world. And we can help our kids learn to do this well. I am determined to give my kids all the tools they need to be leaders, to influence others positively in their world.

Like you, I share the feelings most parents have as they raise their children. Apprehension. Fear. Overwhelming responsibility. Lack of time. When our children were younger, my wife, Pam, and I worked to explain the answers to their questions. When they still didn't understand after long discourses, we found ourselves saying to them, "No, you don't get it." Then, we would proceed down another path to help them understand. Recently, my eight-year-old son, Jonathan, attempted to explain something going on at school to me. This time, I had several questions. When

I continued to probe, he retorted: "No, Dad, you don't get it." Touché. The tables have been turned.

The fact is, sometimes I don't get it. I am guilty of making snap judgments and sizing things up too quickly. This doesn't work successfully with kids. Working with students is an adventure; every day brings some new challenge. We can't presume we understand everything based on first impressions. And it begins the moment they are born. Thomas Hutzler relates a story about a father who learned this the hard way:

> As ham sandwiches go, it was perfection. A thick slab of ham, a fresh bun, crisp lettuce, and plenty of expensive, light brown gourmet mustard. The corners of my jaw were aching in anticipation. I carried it to the picnic table in our backyard, picked it up with both hands but was stopped by my wife, suddenly at my side.
>
> "Hold Johnny (our six-week-old son) while I get my sandwich," she said. I had him balanced between my left elbow and shoulder and was reaching for my sandwich again, when I noticed a streak of mustard on my fingers.
>
> I love mustard.
>
> I had no napkin.
>
> I licked it off.
>
> It wasn't mustard.
>
> No man ever put a baby down faster. It was the first and only time I have sprinted with my tongue protruding. With a washcloth in each hand, I did the sort of routine shoeshine boys do, only I did it on my tongue. Later (after she stopped crying from laughing so hard), my wife said, "Now you know why they call the mustard 'Poupon.'"

I want you to have fun reading this book. I'll do my best to make it enjoyable. You'll find that I'm much like you—I want to foster the gifts inside my children. With this book, my goal is to provide some practical tools (principles and ideas) for your toolbox as you attempt to nurture and develop the leadership qualities already inside of your sons and daughters. I will furnish leadership principles for them, mentoring principles for you, and lots of ideas for how you can invest in them and develop them. I'll tell stories to illustrate how the principles work and help you to evaluate how you and your child are developing them. I hope to give you a plan to develop a young leader.

By the way, this book isn't only for parents. Perhaps you are a coach, teacher, pastor, or university staff member. I'm writing to anyone who wants to bring out the leader inside a young person. With that said, let me paint you a broad picture of what I've laid out in this book.

The first section of this book provides insights on what you need to know about connecting with kids in this culture. You need to understand their world. I will unpack the "mosaic" culture in which this generation lives. I'll try to give you tools to reach them.

The second section provides the fundamentals you will need to discuss with your kids if they're to understand leadership. I encourage you to help them understand these principles, measure their growth, and do the "life purpose" exercise.

The third section covers how to seize teachable moments and when to pass along the principles during the natural junctions of a typical day. You'll be able to map out a plan to make deposits in their hearts.

The final section deals with how to mentor your kids in leadership intentionally and effectively. When you implement the principles, there will be a method to your madness. The adventure awaits—let's get going!

PART 1

WHAT YOU NEED TO KNOW

1

So You Want Your Child to Be a Leader

It is easier to shape a child than to rebuild an adult.
—Dr. James Dobson

THE ATMOSPHERE IN THEIR NICE, suburban home grew tense. Jeff had come home early from the office to find his wife, Susan, clearly upset and unsure of what to do. Moments earlier, their son, Chris, had phoned home for his mother to come and get him from school. This was the fourth day in a row he'd called to come home early. Chris, a fifth-grader who suffered from asthma and made poor grades, usually called home by 11:00 A.M. because he was being bullied and teased by his classmates. What were Jeff and Susan supposed to do? Why didn't they get a manual on parenting when their son was born? They were not prepared for days like these.

That evening at the dinner table they listened to Chris whine about being different, moan about his asthma, and relate how hard it was to get along with the other kids in his school. While the situation had been percolating for months, everything now came to a head. Life was not working for this eleven-year-old kid. Later that night, Susan and Jeff tried to figure out how to fix the situation. Susan's natural instinct was to waltz down to that school and talk to the principal, to fight back, and to protect her boy.

Both agreed that might be the quickest solution to the problem—but probably not the best one. Their son's struggle was not only because of the teasing and the asthma, but also because he wanted to be in charge. And right now, he was anything but in charge of his situation. He was uncompromising, sensitive, and had a strong sense of justice, even for other kids in the school. Now, he was becoming a victim and getting attention for it. If Susan spoke to the principal and fixed the problem of the teasing, she wouldn't help Chris in the long run. He would remain a victim and never become the leader his parents knew was inside of him.

Jeff and Susan decided they would work with Chris to help him deal with the situation effectively. They would give him tools to solve his own problems and help others as well. They began to have conversations with Chris to help him to see what was happening. They explained the difference between a victim and a leader. They helped him think through and interpret each of his school-time situations. They helped him read people, strengthen his debate skills, and see others with his heart—to look past their faults and see their needs. They told him stories of how other kids handled problems and took a stand. They even taught him the influence of silence.

This was a bonding season for Jeff, Susan, and Chris. Over the course of a year, the results were nothing short of dramatic—Chris began to be the person he was born to be. His grades went up. He became confident. He slowly became the top opinion leader in his class. When his family moved to a new city, the principal wrote a letter to his new school, describing Chris this way: "I have been in education for twenty-five years. I have never seen a child come into a school and take over the hearts of his peers like Chris. He is a leader."

Jeff and Susan are friends of mine. They don't claim to be experts in parenting. They were even hesitant about my including their story in this book. I wanted to because they illustrate the profound difference a parent can make when they play offense—not just defense—in the home. Jeff and Susan saw leadership potential in their son, Chris. I see some in my kids. My guess is you see some in your kids, too. That's why you picked up this book.

Let's reflect for a moment on our motives and our goals. What might happen if you and I became proactive about drawing out the potential in our children? What if we learned to play offense, as a parent, and coach them in leadership? What kind of difference would it make if we actually had a plan? These are great questions that all have answers. I believe our coaching can make all the difference in the world.

WHY YOUR KID?

If you are like me, you want your kid to influence the world he or she lives in, rather than merely be influenced by it. As they grow older, you want to see them make a difference, not just make a living. There are a variety of reasons for wanting to nurture the leader in your child.

I sat down recently and asked myself this very question. Why do I want my kids, Bethany and Jonathan, to be leaders? What is my motivation? Let me offer you some reasons:

1. Because I See Leadership Gifts Inside of Them.

I believe every child is a potential leader. They may not become the next Lee Iacocca, Norman Schwarzkopf, or Mother Teresa—but I believe inside every kid lies great potential to influence other people. Leadership begins with influence. Sociologists tell us today that even the most introverted people will influence ten thousand others in an average lifetime. Wow. It makes me wonder: How many people will my kids influence? I see some leadership gifts inside both of my children. Bethany has a compassionate heart for the hurting. She is discerning and loves to assist people in need. Jonathan loves to communicate and to build relationships. Both of them enjoy helping others do the right thing. I want to help them help others effectively.

2. Because I See the Needs of the World in Which They Live.

Ever since I took a leadership position twenty-two years ago, I have seen a world crying out for good leaders. George Barna, founder of the Barna Research Group, warned us three years ago that America was in a leadership crisis. Management guru, Peter Drucker, told us the same thing in the 1980s. Kids can't always look to political leaders as models. The moral fiber of Washington was a joke through the 1990s. They can't always look to athletes to be models. Millionaire sports stars reveal their true "cause" as they selfishly whine over salary caps with millionaire team owners. Often, kids cannot even look to religious leaders as examples of integrity, character, and moral leadership. In the words of seventeen-year-old Josh Lee in a letter to the *Chicago Sun-Times,* "the biggest problem [we have] is the example adults show kids today."[1]

3. Because I Want to Give Them a Head Start.

I am part of a generation of parents who pays more attention to raising their kids than any other for the last hundred years. This new generation is getting tremendous attention and reinforcement. In 1991, a *Washington Post* headline read: "Educational Toys Are Spelled H-O-T as Parents Seek to Give Kids an Edge." Whether it is good or bad, kids today own twice as many things as they did thirty years ago. Parents today don't want their children to be disadvantaged in any way.

I'm not the first parent to say I want to give my kids the advantages I never had. I want to help them make it as far as they can go. A friend of mine said to me recently: "I am almost paranoid about not spending enough time with my kids. I just don't want to be a bad dad."

4. Because I Don't Want Them to Miss Reaching Their Potential.

As I look at my kids, both inside and out, I want them to capitalize on the potential that lies inside of them and around them. Currently, there is a coming together of talent, opportunity, and desire nationwide that is rare indeed. We have a generation of kids who want to seize the moment. The Prudential Community Awards are given out each year to kids who exhibit exceptional leadership and service to their community. Last year, thousands of names were entered to win. Each year seems to set a new record. Unlike the depressed Generation X of the 1980s, this new batch of kids sees the mess that the world is in—but feels compelled to change it. They want to use their gifts, technology, and the world's hunger for hope. What a great time in history to nurture a leader!

5. Because My Kids Are Hungry for an Adult Mentor.

For more than ten years, the buzzword "mentor" has been in vogue, but the concept is more than a mere fad. This emerging generation is asking for adult mentors, hungry to be coached. My son overheard me talking to a friend about this a couple of years ago. He was only six years old, but he must have understood what we said. As I tucked him into bed that night, he asked me: "Daddy, will you be my mentor?" Those are words every father loves to hear.

It is not uncommon for this generation of kids also to seek mentors from their grandparents' generation. They often pursue help on their own, and as they spot their own weaknesses, they'll seek out specialists in those areas. Donna Shalala, former Secretary for the U.S. Department of Health and Human Services, affirmed recently, "Most teenagers are making good choices—focusing on their futures and saying no to anything that would jeopardize their dreams." This is quite a shift from fifteen to twenty years ago. In later chapters, I will share ideas on how you can effectively mentor your kids in leadership and help them uncover their God-given purpose in life.

6. Because I Want Them to Influence Rather Than Be Influenced.

We don't want our kids doing something "just because everyone else is doing it." Like Jeff and Susan, we don't want our child to be a victim of their circumstances. We want them to make up their own minds, make their own choices. Just yesterday, I had a talk with my kids about mirrors and portraits, frogs and kettles, thermometers and thermostats.

Mirrors only do one thing; they reflect whatever is in front of them. I want my kids to be a portrait rather than a mirror. I want them to make their own statement to the world, not merely reflect what the world is saying.

If you try to cook a frog in a kettle of boiling water, he will jump right out. However, if you put the frog in a kettle of cool water and slowly turn the temperature up, he will sit there until he boils to death. Why? Because his body temperature will rise slowly with the water. He never notices that he only reflects the temperature of his environment until it is too late.

On a similar theme, a thermometer tells you what the temperature is, but a thermostat sets the temperature. I want my kids to be thermostats (leaders who influence), not thermometers (those who merely inform others).

7. Because Their Generation Is Primed to Make a Difference.

When my daughter Bethany was eleven, she and I were on a "date" together. Dates always give us lots of father/daughter discussion time. As we ate together, I asked her about her dreams for the future, and we began to talk about her career. When I asked her what she wanted to do when she grew up, she responded: "Well, I can't make up my mind between three jobs—but I know I'm going to change the world."

Much of the despair and pessimism from the last twenty years has been replaced with a new optimism and a bent for getting involved by this new generation. In the 1960s, the baby boomers believed they would change the world—but they opted to work outside the system, in rebellion. This new generation shares their beliefs but not their methods; they are working within existing systems and organizations for the greater good.

8. Because We Are at a Critical Point in History.

As we enter the twenty-first century, we are at a crossroads. Will our kids be ready for the future? Technology has made global communication expedient, and change is happening at a rate that would make our grandparents' heads spin. One person can make a move and impact millions before the day is over!

In addition, we've changed the way we think. We no longer assume that any truths are "self-evident" as our forefathers did in the Declaration of Independence. For many, truth is relative. There is greater diversity in the American population, but also greater tolerance and greater desire to experience community. More generations are alive at the same time than ever before. What a time to be alive! What a time to raise kids!

Dr. John C. Maxwell said, "Our world needs leaders who know the way, go the way, and show the way." I think we are in need of leaders now more than at any other point during my lifetime.

---

9. Because I Want to Leave a Legacy in Them.

My friend Reggie Joiner differentiates between leaving an inheritance and leaving a legacy: An inheritance is something you leave for your kids, and a legacy is something you leave in them. I want to proactively build character, decision-making skills, vision, relational skills, and courage in my kids so that they can carry those qualities into the next generation with them. Neal Postman, Culture Critic for N.Y.U., said, "Children are the living messages we send into a time we will not see."

A boy living in New Jersey waits expectantly every year for the mailman to deliver a special letter to him on his birthday. His father, while dying of a terminal disease, knew his son would not have the benefit of his personal guidance and help as he grew into manhood. So, he wrote the young boy a letter for each year and left instructions for the letters to be sent so they would arrive annually on the proper date. A final envelope containing words of fatherly direction and advice will also be given to his son on his wedding day. The influence of the father is being felt long after he is gone.

This final reason is probably the most important reason of all to me. I am doing my best to leave a living legacy, with each day I'm given, as I invest in my children.

WHAT ARE YOU AFRAID OF?

There are a variety of fears that surface when we talk about parenting and mentoring our kids. We all feel a bit inadequate about parenting, not to mention developing leadership qualities in our kids. Honestly, I wonder if I have what it takes to mentor my kids in leadership. Where do we find the time? Where do we find the resources? Where do we find the insight in our own lives to pass on to them?

I had to face two realities. First, I cannot lead my kids any further than where I have grown myself. We teach what we know, but we reproduce what we are. We cannot build a better leader than we are without help. Here's the good news. This book will coach you as you coach your kids. Besides, our goal is not to clone ourselves but to foster the leadership gifts our kids already have.

Second, none of us is perfect. We will make mistakes, yet we must resolve that this will not stop us from doing all we can to develop leadership potential in our children. John Crosby put the cookies on the bottom shelf when he said: "A mentor is a brain to pick, a shoulder to cry on, and a kick in the seat of the pants." We all have a brain, a shoulder, and a foot. Let's do what we can with what we have. We can outsource the rest as our kids outgrow us.

I am not predicting your kid will become the next Nelson Mandela or Elizabeth Dole, but I do believe you can exercise positive influence if you will help them do six things:

1. Know themselves

2. Develop their gift

3. Find their passion

4. Value people

5. Learn perseverance

6. Pursue excellence

Be encouraged—your job is not to force your child into a role they are not cut out for, but to help them to reach their potential.

LEARNING FROM HISTORY

Have you noticed how many young people have engineered great changes throughout history? Youth have held central roles in the radical shifts of some spiritual and social movements for centuries:

- Josiah became a king in ancient Israel when he was eight years old. By the time he was a teenager, he had matured into a solid leader among the Hebrew people and had brought about significant reforms in the land.

- Joan of Arc led three thousand French knights to victory in the Battle of Orleans when she was only seventeen years old.

- John Wesley started his "holy club" to breathe life into an apathetic church as a teenager. He and his brother, Charles, were passionate about reforming British society in the days of the bloody French and American revolutions. By the time he was seventeen, he founded the organization that became the Methodist church.

- Mozart never attended a proper school but instead was taught by his father, a musician. By the age of six, Mozart composed his first symphony and was an accomplished performer in three instruments. By thirteen, Mozart's father took him on a tour through Italy where he was exposed to the music of another culture. As a teenager, he broke new ground as a professional composer and performer.

- Louis Braille accidentally pierced his eye when he was three, and within two years he went blind. At age ten, he was sent to Paris to the National Institute for Blind Children. Although he was a good student, he was dissatisfied because he couldn't read. By age twelve, he had created a reading method for the blind using a pattern of six raised dots to represent letters and symbols. At fifteen, he showed his six-dot method to his classmates, who liked it. In 1852 the world adopted the boy's method as a standard: the Braille system.

- And how about Albert Einstein? Although he flunked math twice in school, it was because he was ahead of his time. He wrote his first paper on the theory of relativity when he was sixteen.

- Bill Gates was nineteen years old when he formed Microsoft with his friend Paul Allen. Two years later, youngster Steven Jobs and Steven Wozniak began The Apple Computer Company, launching The Apple II in 1977. All four young men were primed and ready to orchestrate change because they were not stuck in a rut or routine.

- Tiger Woods started playing golf when he was three. By the time he was a teen, he was good enough to capture the attention of the press. He was known nationwide by the time he reached college, and he had an influential voice, particularly with other young people.

Ordinary young people have been impacting their everyday world as well. When he was eleven years old, Trevor Ferrell was doing his homework in front of the TV in his Philadelphia home. A documentary came on about the homeless in that city. He was so moved, he talked to his parents about it at dinner that evening. His mom and dad suggested they pray and give some money to help the homeless—but they could tell Trevor was determined to do more than that.

They agreed to take a trip downtown, to allow Trevor to give a blanket and a sack lunch to a homeless person on the streets. His parents quietly hoped this would make him feel better. It only fueled his passion to serve the homeless and the poor. Soon, Trevor had campaigned to start an outreach to feed and clothe the needy in the city—and volunteers joined in. By the time he was a teenager, Trevor led this team of volunteers, who provided food, blankets, beds, and warmth to those in need. And it all began with a sixth-grade kid.

A Divine Movement.

One reason for this groundswell of activism today is the growing spiritual passion of our kids. This new generation of kids thinks, talks, and does more about their faith than older people realize. In 1990, there were no registered prayer circles or clubs in U.S. public high schools. Now, there are more than ten thousand of them. In one poll, teens cited religion as the second strongest influence in their lives, just behind parents but ahead of teachers, boyfriends and girlfriends, peers, and the media. It is popular to pursue spiritual things. The increase in spiritual vitality has grown from the baby boomers to Generation X to the millennial generation. Kids pray in circles, wear WWJD wristbands, and meet in clubs after school to discuss spiritual growth. There is a collective sense that they are to make the world a better place.

What Are We to Do?

All of this is either scary or exciting to you. Maybe both. You can equip your kids to be the leaders they are gifted to be. You can do it—I am commissioning you to be their leadership mentor.

One night, a father and his five-year-old son decided to take a walk along a muddy road after a long rain. The boy's mother agreed to let them go, but only if he was careful not to get any mud on his pants. Unfortunately, within the first few minutes, the five-year-old had fallen into a pothole and gotten mud everywhere. Without a second thought, he looked up at his father and asked: "Dad—why don't you watch where I'm going?"

That's a good question for every mentor and every parent.

Reflect and Respond

1. What are your reasons for wanting to nurture the leader in your child?

2. What do you see in them that makes you think they might influence others?

3. List one step you could take to encourage your child to make a difference in their world.

2

THE MILLENNIAL GENERATION AND THE POSTMODERN WORLD

May you live in interesting times.
—CHINESE PROVERB

WHEN THE PHONE RANG, a tiny voice answered, "Hello?"

"Hello, what's your name?" a gentleman caller asked.

"My name is Jimmy, and I'm four years old!"

"Well, that's wonderful, Jimmy," replied the man. "Is your daddy home?"

"Yes . . . but he's real busy," whispered Jimmy.

"Oh, I see. Well, is your mommy home?"

"Yeah, but she's real busy, too."

"I see. Are there any other adults home that I could talk to?" inquired the man.

"The police are here. But they're real busy, too."

"Oh my goodness. Well, is anyone else there?"

"Yeah, the firemen are here. But . . . they're busy, too."

"Wow! Your dad, your mom, the police and the fire department are all there? What are they all doing, Jimmy?"

Jimmy smiled. "They're looking for me!"

In many ways, this is a picture of us. Adults, whether sociologists or parents, scurry about trying to identify where this new generation of kids is and what they think. It is difficult to know for sure. What we do know is the millennial generation, kids born between 1984 and 2001, is different from their predecessors: the builders, the boomers, and the busters. The daily news my mom and dad remember is ancient history to my kids because so much has changed. The millennials are growing up in a world that is radically different from what we knew:

- They were the first generation to be born into Luvs, Huggies, and Pampers
- They were the first infants to ride in a car with the sign "Baby on board"
- John Lennon and John Belushi have always been dead
- There have always been women on the Supreme Court and traveling in space
- They grew up with Microsoft, IBM, PCs, Nutrasweet, and CDs
- They never knew Madonna when she was "like a virgin"
- Strikes by highly paid athletes have been a routine part of professional sports
- The moonwalk is a Michael Jackson dance step, not a Neil Armstrong giant step
- The term "adult" has come to mean "dirty"
- They have spent more than half their life with Bart Simpson
- President Kennedy's assassination is as relatively insignificant to them as Lincoln's
- They have never feared a nuclear war
- They have probably never dialed a phone
- The terms "roll down your window" and "you sound like a broken record" have to be explained

Regardless of what we think about the world in which our kids are growing up, one thing is for sure. If we hope to mentor our kids and foster their leadership gifts—we must understand how they think and the world they live in. According to the U.S. Census Office, the world's population on December 31, 2000, was just under 6.12 billion people, and 2.1 billion are currently part of a global youth culture. By 2025, one quarter of the world's population will have been born between 1982 and 2002. You probably know at least one of those kids.

The world is different now than when we grew up. In many ways, I feel like a stranger in a strange land. I am an immigrant. My kids are the natives. They are at home in this new world. They have always lived with fast-paced change. They are not confused with split-second images flashing across TV commercials. They can process visuals much faster than their parents can. They have grown up accustomed to multitasking. In fact, they like all their senses involved. They are used to watching music on TV or computers, not merely listening to it. They get bored quickly. They like things to move and change. And while all of this may wear out their parents and grandparents, it has sharpened them up. Research has shown that this generation is already actively involved in community problem solving. They want to be part of the answer. They want to fix the world.

I heard a cute story that illustrates the nature of this new generation. A young mother had experienced a difficult morning. Her dishwasher wasn't working, a kitchen light had burned out, the bills were bigger than she had expected that month, and to top it off, the washing machine had flooded the utility room floor. As she set a bowl of creamed peas in front of her one-and-a-half-year-old son, she fell apart. She slumped over and began to cry right in front of his high chair. The toddler watched her for a moment, and then he grabbed the pacifier out of his mouth and offered it to her.

FIVE GENERATIONS

It is important that we get a big-picture perspective on this new generation. On the following page I've provided a chart that summarizes the last five generations of Americans. As you look it over, you will see their differences

Leadership issue	Seniors	Builders	Boomers	Busters	Millennials
1. Era They Were Born	1900–1928	1929–1945	1946–1964	1965–1983	1984–2001
2. Worldview	Manifest destiny	Be grateful you have a job	You owe me	Relate to me	Life is a cafeteria
3. Attitude to Authority	Respect them	Endure them	Replace them	Ignore them	Choose them
4. Role of Relationships	Long-term	Significant	Limited: useful	Central; caring	Global
5. Value Systems	Traditional	Conservative	Self-based	Media	Shop around
6. Role of Career	Loyalty	Means for living	Central focus	Irritant	A place to serve
7. Schedules	Responsible	Mellow	Frantic	Aimless	Volatile
8. Technology	What's that?	Hope to outlive it	Master it	Enjoy it	Employ it
9. Market They Introduce	Commodities	Goods	Services	Experiences	Transformations
10. View of Future	Uncertain	Seek to stabilize	Create it!	Hopeless	Optimistic

and how each reacts to the previous generation's mind-set. George Barna, founder and president of the Barna Research Group, Ltd., inspired this chart. As new information has emerged, I have added it to the chart to make it more current. The categories "Worldview," "Market They Introduce," and "View of Future" are especially helpful to understand the perspective of the millennials and how they differ from former generations.

Their Worldview.

The *millennials* embrace a different perspective on life than previous generations. The *seniors*, or GI generation, entered the world one hundred years ago. They embarked on a new century with a sense of destiny but were the silent generation. Next, came the *builders*. They endured the Great Depression and embraced the attitude "be grateful you have a job." They learned to be frugal and cautious with their resources. Next came the *baby boomers*, the huge, pig-in-the-python generation that popularized the entitlement philosophy. Boomers felt the world owed them a good life—at least, that's what the TV commercials told them. This philosophy didn't make for good marriages or stable careers, and the kids born to boomer parents paid for it. *Generation X* (or the baby busters) followed the boomers and felt abandoned. Their paradigm became "relate to me." They long for relationships that give them hope and help.

Finally, the millennial generation has come of age. For them, life is a cafeteria. They pick and choose everything, from music to religion. They are deeply spiritual as a whole, but they mix and match their belief systems, often claiming multiple citizenship in several of the more than 2,100 religious groups in the U.S. today.[1]

All of this means that we must help them make wise decisions in a world saturated with options. With so many choices in front of them, the temptation will be to simply do what everyone else is doing and defer the decision-making power they have.

The Market They Introduce.

The millennials also introduce a new market to the economy. Authors James Gilmore and Joseph Pine, in *Work Is Theatre and Every Business a Stage*, describe the different generations in market terms.

The senior generation bought and sold commodities. On their birthdays, their moms would make them cakes from scratch, with fresh eggs, milk, and sugar. (Many millennials don't know what the term "made from scratch" means!)

The builder generation bought and sold goods. For the first time, moms could buy a cake mix from Betty Crocker. Moms still baked cakes in their own ovens, but now food was processed. For the first time, consumers expected a streamlined process.

Next, the baby boomers introduced the service economy. Boomer consumers expect to be served—others were paid to provide lawn care, housecleaning, and car washing in order to save precious time. For their birthdays, their moms would drive over to bakeries or Baskin-Robbins stores to buy cakes. Moms were willing to spend more money to save the more valuable time.

When Generation X arrived, our world entered the "experience" economy. People buy and sell experiences such as Starbucks coffee, Disney World, or Virtual Reality. On their children's birthdays, simple cakes are no longer enough—parents take children to Chuck E. Cheese's for "an experience." Children expect all of their senses to be involved in all aspects of life.

As the twenty-first century progresses, Gilmore and Pine predict that the new generation will buy not only experiences but also transformations. Vendors will soon offer parents a menu of parties, transforming experiences centered on themes such as education, spiritual growth, or relationships that are brought directly to homes. Children will learn and be "transformed" at these parties.[2]

As the market evolves, the standard is being raised. I cannot merely lecture my kids and expect them to genuinely learn. This new generation has higher expectations; they want an experience that transforms.

Their View of the Future.

The millennial generation also views the future differently. The seniors felt uncertain about it, the builders sought to stabilize it, and the boomers arrogantly began to create it. Generation X felt hopeless and helpless since their world was so messed up. Yet, despite a world still full of problems and complexities, the millennial generation is optimistic as a whole. Many actually believe they can change the world. Three of four teens think about their future several times a week, many millennials noting it is easy to find fault in the world but tough to act on to change it. One teen said, "The fundamental difference between Boomers, Xers and us Millennials is that older generations resist the idea that things can get better. They see problems, get depressed, complain about them, and raise us to get by in a harsh world. All the while, they refuse to take an extra leap of optimism necessary to change things. It's easy to find fault in the world. It's tough to act on that."[3]

As the twentieth century came to a close, it was easy to see why a new bunch of kids could be optimistic. The economy was good and technology was booming. Kids got lots of attention, and the government began to make them a priority. Moms and dads even focused on being good parents. During these formative years, this young generation got the idea that maybe the future might be bright as well.

For parents, this is exciting news. We must capitalize on this optimism. We must ride the wave of their spirit that believes they can make a difference. We will have to corral them from time to time and give them a dose of realism, but it's sure easier than motivating a generation full of cynical attitudes.

Landmark Events.

In 1999, authors Neil Howe and William Strauss surveyed the high school class of 2000 and reported their findings in *Millennials Rising.* In response to the question, "What event made the biggest impression on you?" this class of teenagers gave the following list of events, in order:

1. Columbine shooting

2. War in Kosovo

3. Oklahoma City bombing

4. Princess Di's death

5. Clinton impeachment trial

6. O. J. Simpson trial

7. Rodney King riots

8. Lewinsky scandal

9. Fall of Berlin Wall

10. McGwire / Sosa home run race[4]

The Columbine High School massacre, a grim rite of passage for many students, scored the highest. Fourteen of their peers and one teacher died in the worst of a series of gunfire tragedies (including those in Arkansas, Kentucky, Oregon, Mississippi, and California). In the wake of these shootings, millennial kids candidly acknowledge the role played by peer pressure. They began to ostracize outsiders and call for community. They had had enough. Columbine seemed to bring conviction to their hearts. Instead of causing them to cower in fear (as many of their parents have done), millennials have determined to become agents for change.

The two gunmen failed to do what they intended to do to their classmates. Students at Columbine and nationwide have come through more firmly tied to their beliefs. Jennifer Pierce, a student at Columbine, said after the massacre, "No matter where those guys fired, they would have hit someone who had high hopes for the future."[5] Ironically, the tragedy didn't depress them. What's more, the May/June issue of *Group Magazine* reported how students have galvanized their faith since that time. The tragedy has had a reverse effect. Cassie Burnall, one of the Columbine victims, has become a peer hero. Why? Because when her life was threatened, she stood for what she believed. It cost her life. Yet, when asked whether they would say "yes" if put into Cassie Burnall's shoes during the Columbine shooting, 49% said definitely "yes," while another 34% said, "I think so." This amazes me. I wonder how my kids would have responded if they were in this position.

LOOKING FOR THE MILLENNIALS

Several studies have been done to capture the beliefs and behaviors of this new generation, such as the ones by Howe and Strauss mentioned above. Coca-Cola did their own survey of 27,000 12- to 19-year-olds from around the world recently. In addition, I did my own survey of three thousand students in 1999. The following is a summary of the conclusions regarding the millennial generation:

1. They feel special.

Movies, government focus, and parents have all contributed to making this generation of kids believe they are vital to our future. *USA Weekend* polled 272,400 teenagers. When asked, "In general, how do you feel about yourself?" 93 percent responded either "really good" (49%) or "kind of good" (44%). Only 6 percent said "not very good"; 1 percent said "bad."[6]

2. They love family.

Millennials rely on family to be a sanctuary from the troubles of the world in which they live. The explosion of child-safety rules and devices has sheltered them. They are the targets of the most sweeping safety movement in history, and their parents have led the way. Kids are enjoying being the focus of attention and development.

3. They are confident.

Millennials believe they can make a difference. With high levels of trust and connection to their parents, they often boast about their generation's power and potential. They are self-reliant and are comfortable acting on what they have been taught by adults. They believe they are responsible for their own success.

4. They are mediavores.

This generation is addicted to media—TV, computer games, video games, CD players, DVD players, and movies. It is not uncommon for them to be doing homework, listening to a CD, watching television, and communicating online simultaneously. They give new definition to the term "multitasking."

5. They are team oriented.

Think about it. They grew up with Barney, played soccer, learned in groups at school, and often wore school uniforms. Unlike previous generations, community accomplishment is more important than individual accomplishments. Millennials are developing solid team instincts and tight peer bonds. Many even date in groups!

6. They are global.

This generation, probably the most mobile group ever, promises to build relationships with people all over the world. They plan to travel worldwide just as they've already done on the Internet. While they enjoy their families much, they don't plan to stay at home because there is too much to experience.

7. They are pressured.

They have been pushed to study hard, avoid personal risks, and take advantage of the opportunities their family has afforded them. Schedules are tight for parents and kids, so they have grown up with the stress of school, soccer league, Cub Scouts, youth group at church, and increased homework after school.

8. They are harmonious.

For the first time in decades, this young generation is cooperative and conventional. They take pride in improving their behavior and are more comfortable with traditional values than any generation in memory. Millennials believe social rules help society go forward. They believe earlier generations were too selfish.

9. They are generous.

The millennials not only enjoy accomplishment, they enjoy giving away their resources and serving their communities. Fifty percent of teenagers are active in community service today. They want to help others and leave the world a better place than they found it. Even at an early age, they seem to care.

10. They are optimistic achievers.

They may be the best-educated, best-behaved adults in the nation's history. They are full of hope. They believe they can make a difference. Unlike Gen Xers, they are not pessimistic or cynical. They love to laugh and have fun and appear to be genuinely happy. Their optimism drives their behavior.

My family lived in Aurora, Colorado, for three years. I will never forget hearing about an elementary school in town that was researching the atrocities in Sudan, Africa. They read about its history and its current events. According to Robert Hoffman, they quickly discovered Sudan's slave trade. One of the children said, "What are we going to do about this?" The group of fourth and fifth graders collected money to buy back slaves in the Sudan. They asked the question and acted on their answer. This would have been unimaginable fifteen years ago—boomers would have gotten high and contemplated it, and Xers would have written angst-filled songs about it. The millennials are doing something about it. When asked why the "leaders" aren't doing anything, a child replied, "If they can't . . . we will."

WILL THEY REBEL?

A natural question might be: Don't all teens rebel at some point? What can we expect from this group of youngsters as they come of age? Won't they stray from their parents' generation and become nonconformists?

The answer, of course, is yes. Many of them will. But the millennials' rebellion will be against the trend of earlier generations, which has always been the pattern. They will be anti-boomer and de-Xed. Seventeen-year-old Chris Loyd wrote, "The best way to rebel for me is to dress formally all the time, respect my elders, love my country and drive a used Toyota, instead of the prerequisite SUV."[7]

According to Howe and Strauss, in 1998, PRIMEDIA/Roper surveyed national youth. Teens identified the top four possible causes of problems in America as selfishness, lack of respect for law and authority, wrongdoing by politicians, and lack of parental discipline. Hmmmm. This sounds more like a set of great-grandparents responding than a group of sixteen-year-olds.

GROWING UP IN A POSTMODERN WORLD

There is another factor we will have to deal with as we attempt to connect with this younger generation. While the millennial generation has many surprisingly positive ingredients, the world in which they are growing up is daunting. Sociologists believe that just prior to the birth of the millennial generation, our culture moved from modern to postmodern thought. Postmodernism is a worldview that's been percolating and increasing in popularity for the last forty years. For some parents, this new way of thinking represents the biggest challenge for them as they try to raise their children today. Difficult to describe, postmodernism is easier to define by clarifying what it is not.

Modernism began with the Enlightenment. Centuries ago, people began to feel that through science and intellectual integrity, the world's problems could be solved. Scientific method became king. Truth was objective and, if looked for, could be found. The men who framed the Declaration of Independence described the feeling of the day: "We hold these truths to be self-evident . . . "

Postmodernism is a reaction to modernism. Relativity, not reason, became king. Friedrich Nietzsche put it well, "There are no facts—only interpretations." Those who embrace postmodern thinking pursue the freedom to express themselves. The power of story or narrative overrides the power of empirical evidence. Tolerance is cherished. Nothing is known for sure. The spiritual world is very real, and God is whoever you want him to be.

MODERN	POSTMODERN
1. HUMANISM Man is the measure of all things.	**1. FATALISM** I have no real control over what happens.
2. ABSOLUTE TRUTH Truth is rational and we will find it.	**2. RELATIVE TRUTH** Truth is relative; each has his own reality.
3. SCIENCE Science is ultimate and will deliver us.	**3. TECHNOLOGY** Technology is our servant and friend.
4. ENLIGHTENMENT I want facts; give me empirical evidence.	**4. NARRATIVE** Tell me your story; give me a picture.
5. UNIVERSAL VALUES Ethics are self-evident and universal.	**5. TOLERANCE** We should be tolerant of everyone's values.
6. MATERIALISM I only believe in what I can see or touch.	**6. SPIRITUALISM** I believe in spiritual realities beyond me.
7. INDIVIDUALISM I am my own person.	**7. COMMUNITY** I am part of interdependent relationships.

The Millennials and the Postmodernists Are Not the Same.

As a parent, I had to come to grips with the fact that my kids are growing up in a postmodern world. At the same time, I now see a distinction. The millennial generation and the postmodern world in which they live are not synonymous. What we have is an emerging youth generation that is optimistic, spiritual, and ambitious who happen to be growing up in a postmodern culture that doesn't always share their optimism. Both will impact the other, and no doubt, the postmodern mind will modify some of the youthful optimism of the millennials. You will find yourself wanting to instill values in your child—values that will enhance his or her future leadership. The challenge will be attempting to do this in a society that doesn't share those values, and teaches that all values are equal, truth being relative. We can't know anything for sure. There is no definite right and wrong. This will be confusing to a millennial.

THE CHALLENGE BEFORE US

I believe there has never been a more exciting time to nurture the leader in your child. The opportunities and challenges we face are awesome and intimidating. You are well aware of the treasure you have in each of your children. And for a few years, you get to influence your children. For a while, you will likely be your children's greatest influence. But it will cost you. Oh, boy, will it cost you. I just believe it is worth it—nurturing children to be the best leaders they can be is the wisest investment anyone can make.

The government recently calculated the cost of raising a child from birth to age eighteen. The price came to $160,140 for a middle-income family. Talk about sticker shock! That figure doesn't even touch college tuition. For those with kids, that price tag leads to wild fantasies about all the things we could have bought, all the places we could have traveled, all the money we could have banked if not for "little Billy." For others, that number might confirm the decision to remain childless. But $160,140 isn't so bad if you break it down. It translates into $8,896.66 a year, $741.38 a month, or $171.08 a week. That's a mere $24.44 a day. Just over a dollar an hour. Still, you might think the best financial advice says don't have children if you want to be rich.

I think it is just the opposite. What do you get for your $160,140?

- Naming rights. First, middle, and last.
- Glimpses of God every day.
- Giggles under the covers every night.
- More love than your heart can hold.
- Butterfly kisses and Velcro hugs.

- Endless wonder over rocks, ants, clouds, and warm cookies.

- A hand to hold, usually covered with jam.

- A partner for blowing bubbles, flying kites, and building sand castles.

- Someone to laugh yourself silly with no matter what the boss said or how your stocks did.

For $160,140 you get to be a hero. In the eyes of a young child, you rank right up there with God. You have the power to heal a boo-boo, scare away monsters under the bed, patch a broken heart, police a slumber party, ground them forever, and raise a young man or young woman to be a world changer. You also get to love them without limits, so one day they will, like you, love without counting the cost.

Reflect and Respond

1. What are the differences between our world and your child's world?

2. Does your child reflect any of the characteristics of the millennial generation?

3. How can you capitalize on the optimism and confidence of this new generation?

3

BECOMING RELEVANT IN YOUR KID'S WORLD

We must use what is cultural to say what is timeless.
—REGGIE JOINER

"THE SCARIEST THING ABOUT KIDS TODAY," cautions David Sarasohn, columnist for the *San Francisco Examiner,* "is how adults feel about them."[1] I confess, sometimes I am one of those adults who can quickly see what's wrong with my kids. In fact, it's easy for me to negatively stereotype young people as irresponsible, ungrateful, and selfish. Sometimes, these perceptions are based on the fact that kids are growing up in a much different world than we did, one that we don't fully understand. Much of what's positive about this new generation remains hidden behind clouds of doubt and suspicion. People tend to be "down on what they're not up on."

When I was growing up in the 1960s, parents popularized the phrase "generation gap." They moaned about the chasm that existed between themselves and their kids. The two generations struggled to connect but often gave up because the new generation just seemed to be worlds apart from the old one.

Today, you and I are feeling what our parents once felt. Howe and Strauss write, "We cannot help feeling loss when we meet kids who have no memory of the Cold War or the Civil Rights movement, or the long hot summers of Vietnam or Watergate, of Bobby or Martin, of sports stars that earned less than presidents, of gas lines and unemployment lines, of stadiums named after heroes."[2] Kids' faces go blank when you bring up these things.

WHY THE GAP?

As far as I'm concerned, generation gaps exist for two reasons. First, adults forget what it was like to be a kid. Time passes, we age, and eventually we don't know how to speak the language of a six-year-old anymore. One father had a conversation recently with his little boy, Matthew, in their car. Matthew was eating an apple in the back seat when he asked, "Daddy, why is my apple turning brown?"

"Because, Son," the dad explained, "after you ate the skin off, the meat of the apple came into contact with the air, which caused it to oxidize, thus changing its molecular structure and turning it a different color."

There was a long silence. Then, Matthew asked softly, "Daddy, are you talking to me?"

A second reason the generation gap exists is that while we may remember what it was like being a kid, we cling to our own "kid culture," which no longer exists. Most adults get trapped in time. Our memory of youth lingers somewhere in our teens, and that becomes the gauge by which we evaluate youth experience. Unfortunately, the culture we lived in back then is gone. Being sixteen years old today is different than being sixteen years old two decades ago.

For example, kids are growing up faster, and the world is changing at an alarming rate. Pediatricians are seeing seven- and eight-year-old girls with budding breasts and pubic hair—and in some girls as young as five. The fact that the age of menstruation has dropped from 19 to 13 has been well documented—the national average is now age 12.8. While some stress that early development is not necessarily unhealthy at age eight, parents are concerned over the pressures that come as girls fill out. Furthermore, boys are exposed to sex and other adult issues six to seven years earlier now. The issues my son and daughter are talking about in elementary and middle school—I wasn't talking about until high school! Kids' bodies may be ready for sex earlier these days, but they are not emotionally prepared for it. Physical maturity does not equal emotional maturity.

GOING SOLO

Newsweek magazine featured a cover article on teens, May 8, 2000, titled "A World of Their Own." Sharon Begley writes that for the first time, "a portrait of the millennial generation is emerging. They were born at a time when the very culture was shifting to accommodate them—changing tables in restrooms, 'baby-on-board' signs in mini vans. Yet, as a group, [teens] lead lives that are more 'adult-free' than those of previous generations."

According to Patricia Hersch, author of the 1998 book *A Tribe Apart*, this generation of kids has spent more time on their own than any other in recent history. When today's teens are not with their friends, many live in the private, adult-free world of the Web and video games. They often shop, look for a job, do homework, research, e-mail, and talk to friends all on the Internet. The average teen spends thirty-eight hours a week in front of TV or a computer. Data released last year from the Alfred P. Sloan Study of Youth and Social Development found that teens spend 9 percent of their waking hours outside of school with their friends. They spend 20 percent of their waking hours alone. That's nearly 30 percent of their time without an adult around!

While this generation as a whole is optimistic about changing the world, some resent the world their parents have left them. They will capitalize on their time alone—but they secretly long for time with parents.

A CROSS-CULTURAL EXPERIENCE

The challenge is before us. If we want to nurture the leader in our children, we must step into their world. Our goal should not only be to understand their generation, but to connect with them, right where they are. It is the job of the communicator to connect with his or her audience, and not vice versa. If you want to connect with your kid—you must build the bridge and cross it. They have never been your age, but you have been theirs.

In 1987, I traveled to Budapest, Hungary. I met a Hungarian soldier, Adam, on the day I arrived. Adam, a pessimist, had only negative things to say about his world and future. He became my challenge. I decided to work at this relationship until he trusted me to breathe some hope into him. We spent time daily together. We toured the castles of Budapest, sampled food, and shared traditions. I moved outside my comfort zone to demonstrate his value to me. I listened and experienced his life. We began a friendship that has impacted both of us. On the plane ride home, I began to think about why my friendship with Adam was so much work. My conclusion was obvious. It was because we had a cross-cultural relationship. He was Hungarian; I was American. He was an atheist; I was a Christian. He believed in communism; I believed in free enterprise. We were two different people. The relationship was labor intensive because there were two cultures involved.

This is why connecting with another generation is so much work. You and your kid are from two different worlds. In many ways, it is a cross-cultural relationship, which will require more work than a peer relationship. In May 2000, futurist Leonard Sweet taught that if you are over thirty-eight years old, you are an "immigrant" in today's culture. If you are under thirty-eight, you are a "native." People edging into midlife will feel like they are docking at Ellis Island, looking at a whole new world. The media, the movie plots, the technology, and the thinking of the new generation seem just plain odd.

So, what do we do? First, we must be honest. Recognize that their culture is different, even distant, unfamiliar territory. It can be disturbing and confusing to a parent who is unaccustomed to the postmodern world. Also, recognize that their culture is daunting. At times it is intimidating to attempt to connect with, and at other times it seems dangerous. Parents are much more afraid of the damage that can happen to their kids today— especially from drugs, violence, and sexually transmitted diseases—than their kids are. Unfortunately, that is where our kids live—so we have to go there. Second, we must engage the culture. As I interact with parents and teachers, I've noticed three major perspectives on today's culture. See if you identify with any of them.

THREE VIEWS ON CULTURE

1. Isolation.

This view believes that culture is evil and must be avoided. Too many bad things are happening in our world today. Parents who embrace this mindset possess an adversarial, us-against-them mentality. They try to maintain their beliefs by staying as far away from mainstream society as possible so that their kids are not stained by it. Kids become like hermits, hiding in caves of subculture, hoping for the evil to pass or for someone to save them from it. Taken to an extreme, isolationist views cause folks to think like the far right, religious military compounds, who store up weapons and food, and don't trust the government or anyone in a position of authority. They'll just play defense. My question is: If we avoid our culture, how will we ever transform it? We cannot improve what we do not touch.

2. Saturation.

The opposite of isolation, this view believes that culture is everything and we must blend with it. Adults who embrace this almost fatalistic view become victims of both the good and the bad in our society. They feel they can't really change anything, so they might as well just give in and enjoy it. They absorb and are absorbed in all that the media, music, and movies have to offer. This perspective of indiscriminate tolerance of everything can cause our kids to become like chameleons, changing color for each situation they find themselves in. They'll just drift with the current and have no real direction in life. My question is: How can we ever change what is wrong in our society if we merely drift with it? Somewhere along the way, we have to take a stand.

3. Interpretation.

The healthiest perspective of the three, interpretation implies that culture is useful and must be employed to communicate values and truth to the younger generation. Those who embrace this mindset determine to utilize the surroundings to learn and grow, to teach and pass on valuable life lessons. Culture is neither good nor bad in itself. It comprises good and bad elements that must be discerned. We are not in denial—we admit we are in a foreign culture. But we determine to learn the language and to translate it, like a missionary in another country. Good missionary translators do three things: they engage the culture, they explore the culture (to learn from it), and they employ the culture to explain truth. When we do this, our kids, in turn, will be able to interpret the culture for themselves. We must be both adaptable and principle-centered. It's a tricky balance. We must have a handle on our culture, and we must have a handle on the timeless values our kids need to know.

Earl Palmer, in his book *The Enormous Exception*, wrote about the Golden Gate Bridge in San Francisco, which is built directly upon the fault zone of the San Andreas Fault. The secret to its durability is its flexibility that enables it to sway some twenty feet at the center of its one-mile suspension span. But that is not all. By design, every part of the bridge— its concrete roadway, steel railings, and cross beams—is inevitably related from one welded joint to the other up through the vast cable system to two great towers and two great land anchor piers. The towers bear most of the weight, and they are embedded into a rock foundation beneath the sea. The bridge is totally anchored within a firm foundation. This is the secret! Flexibility and foundation.

ENGAGING THE CULTURE

I have determined to engage the culture I live in. I will neither avoid it nor submit to it. I will use it to learn and to teach values to my kids. I was introduced to this lifestyle the hard way, almost twenty years ago. I worked with a youth group at a small church in a small town. I was constantly negotiating between parents and teens over issues such as discipline, curfew, dress codes, and music—especially music. One Sunday night, it all came to a climax for me as I watched an episode of *20/20,* which featured all the members of the heavy metal band, KISS. Do you remember KISS?

They were extremely popular during the late 1970s and early 1980s. They wore bizarre costumes, painted their faces black and white, and sang songs parents did not find helpful as they tried to raise respectful kids.

As I watched the documentary, I became upset. The band members were boasting about their sexual exploits, the drugs and the money they were taking and making. I knew the parents and the teens in my church were watching—and I could foresee World War III breaking out. I decided to turn off the TV and take a walk to cool off. As I walked, I prayed, "Lord, what should I do about this?" I began to think of several "safe" ideas that I could do in response to this dilemma, including holding a seminar for parents and teens on the evils of rock music. Suddenly, I felt that none of these options was good enough. I began to get this nagging feeling that I should do something much more engaging. It was a crazy idea—but I became convinced that I ought to go and talk to KISS! *What might happen,* I thought, *if an ordinary guy like me got the chance to talk to them about the impact they were having on kids, about their spiritual lives, and about the future?*

I discovered that KISS would be in concert that fall in my city. I did my homework on the group, put some things in print for them, and determined to find the hotel where they would stay while in town. My research uncovered them in room 628 of the Camelot Inn. I waited for hours beside the elevators. Finally, at midnight, I took the elevator up to the sixth floor and saw their guard outside of their room. He was huge. Trembling with fear, I approached him, looked him right in the kneecap, and spoke. "Sir, my name is Tim Elmore. I am a youth pastor in town. I am not a groupie or a weirdo, but I would like to have a few minutes to talk to the four members of KISS, if you don't mind."

He grunted as he looked down at me. "It's my job to keep people like you away."

"I know, sir," I responded, "and I know you could do a fine job of that right now, seeing that I am half your size." I paused. "But, if you won't let me talk to them, would you, at least, give them these notes I wrote to them, please?" I handed him the material.

He looked at it, then grew very calm. He could see my concern. "Wow," he said. "What you want to talk about is pretty serious."

"Yes," I replied softly.

"Well, I'm not supposed to tell anyone this," he said. "But every night after their concerts, they go downstairs to the bar for a little nightcap. If you want to join us there at about 2:00 A.M., you can talk to them as long as you'd like."

I smiled, shook his hand, thanked him, and went downstairs to wait for the longest two hours of my life. But it was worth it. The bodyguard, some women, and the four members of KISS entered the bar, and we had the most intriguing conversation. Three of them had already read the material I had given their bodyguard. We talked about their relationship with God, about teens, and about the spiritual complexion of our culture. They seemed totally engaged. They weren't high or drunk or wasted. We even prayed together at the conclusion of our time together. It was amazing.

Since that time, I have seen several positive changes happen in the lives of those band members. No doubt, they are much older now, just as I am. But it has been good to see them use their influence and their money more positively when they did a comeback concert, just a few years ago. More important to me, however, was my personal takeaway. I learned firsthand that it is far better to light a candle than to curse the darkness. Instead of getting mad, why not get busy? Instead of retreating from the culture, why not engage it?

BECOMING RELEVANT

If we hope to develop our kids, we've got to become relevant to this millennial generation. This is the challenge for every parent in every generation. How do we communicate principles that are universal and timeless to a young population that is caught up in today?

Last year, I had an invigorating conversation with Reggie Joiner, founder of the nonprofit organization FamilyWise. He shared with me a definition for the word "relevance":

Relevance is using what is cultural to say what is timeless.

I believe this is critical for us to understand if we hope to nurture the leader in our child. Our generation must cling to the timeless values we know are essential but find ways to pass them on to an ever-changing culture of kids. Ask yourself: What are the essential principles of life you want your kid to know? How will you best transfer those principles to them? What will help them really get it? Your responses will force you to become relevant and to use the right tools to arrive at your goal.

I have been out sailing just two times in my life, and both were learning experiences. (You might say I am "aqua-challenged.") On my second time out, the winds were severe, and I was thankful to have been with an experienced sailor who knew how to negotiate them. I would have given up until they died down. That's when an analogy dawned on me. When the wind is strong, a sailor has three choices: to hold the rope and let the wind take him where he doesn't want to go; to let go of the rope and drift aimlessly along; or to learn to adjust the sails so they will take him where he wants to go. This third option is a picture of relevance. The wind represents our changing culture. A sailor can use the wind or be used by it. The wind can be a friend or a foe depending on what we do with it. Good sailors don't fear the wind; they utilize it.

SEVEN WAYS TO STAY RELEVANT

1. Become a Student of the Culture.

Study the world your kids live in. Listen with more than your ears. Read magazines and newspapers and look for patterns. Interview kids. Learn their language. Watch what they do, what they esteem, and where they go. You might even try to watch an hour of MTV. (I know that may be pushing the envelope a bit!) You will be amazed how quickly you can reach your destination if you learn to adjust your sails and use the wind to help you.

2. Learn to Distinguish What Is Cultural and What Is Timeless.

Both kids and adults struggle with "baptizing" cultural issues from their own generation. Like a missionary in a foreign land, decide what you can do to bridge the gap between cultures. Know what you will die for and what you won't. Like the Golden Gate Bridge, be flexible but stand on your foundation—and pass on that foundation to your kids. For example, my wife and I wrote down six core values that make up our family foundation:

1. Honesty—we want our kids to feel safe being honest with us regardless of the issue

2. Positive attitudes—we believe attitudes are a choice regardless of our circumstances

3. Service to others—we want to generously serve others around us who have needs

4. Responsibility—we want our kids to assume—not avoid—responsibility for their actions

5. Gratitude—we want our kids to be thankful for even the little things they receive

6. Obedience—we want our kids to promptly obey us, even if they don't like the rules

Our goal is for our kids to learn these and put them into practice. It is their leadership foundation. As we learn to teach them, we plan to keep a relevant connection with them. It's not easy, but it's doable. In the next chapter, we'll talk about how to do this.

3. Look for Redemptive Analogies.

I learned this relevant principle from missionary Don Richardson. Every culture and every generation has within it some redemptive analogies—pictures of truth that come out of the culture. They may be situations, events, or people who illustrate a timeless principle. These illustrations can be positive or negative and still be useful. For instance, all of us received a vivid opportunity to talk to our kids about character during the impeachment trial of President Clinton. The lessons had nothing to do with being a Democrat or Republican but had everything to do with the importance of integrity and trust.

4. Create a Leadership Gymnasium.

Once you come up with a redemptive analogy, find or create a "leadership gymnasium"—a place for your children to exercise their leadership muscles. As we mentor our kids, we must find ways to translate good thoughts into practice. This accelerates their learning. Ask the question: What can we do about this principle? Schools are perfect laboratories to teach them to distinguish between what is cultural and what is timeless. I try to help my kids interpret what happens among their peers and be ready for the real world when they are adults. We want them to learn to be "salt and light" to their own generation. This means acting on the values they embrace.

5. Communicate from Their World.

Once we arrive at redemptive analogies and find leadership gymnasiums, we must communicate with our kids. I believe we should always teach from what we have heard from them. My goal is seldom to give them more information. (They usually have plenty of that!) I want them to apply what they know. I try to help them practice what they learn. Transformation comes from application. We don't want them to forget and lose what they have gained.

For instance, when I tuck my kids into bed, we often begin a little exercise I call "making sense of the day." We will talk through anything unusual that may have happened that day, and I ask them if they have any questions or confusion over the way someone acted or what a teacher said, for example. We then interpret together the best way to understand it and answer three questions: What could you have done to help a person? What could you have done to solve a problem? What could you have done to improve a situation?

6. Never Assume That What Worked Yesterday Should Work Today.

Change happens so quickly in our world, we are foolish to assume we can continue to do what we have always done with our kids. They are growing and changing, and their world is growing and changing. We must show creativity and communicate new ideas to mentor to them. As I converse with my kids, I get a sense of how far they are ready to go, and see what connects. My rule of thumb is that their attention span is about the same as their age. My daughter Bethany is thirteen years old—she is good for thirteen minutes. When they show signs of drifting mentally, I know it is time to do something new.

7. Measure Success by Connection, Not Control.

Be sure to measure the right stuff: Our goal is not to control our children's lives but to connect with them so we can give them all the tools they will need to reach their potential. Pay attention to how well you are relating to them; how safe they feel to talk transparently with you; how secure they are with themselves and with your love; how much they feel you understand them; and how much they seem to understand you when you share.

At this point, I encourage you to forge ahead. You are becoming a hero to a young, emerging leader.

Reflect and Respond

1. Would your child consider you relevant to his or her world?

2. How have you engaged your culture rather than blended with it?

3. Name one step you can take to become and stay relevant.

4

Gaining the Keys to Their Hearts

*We must build bridges of relationship that
will bear the weight of truth.*

I will never forget watching the Summer Olympics of 1992. There was one particular competition that was memorable for me. It was the 400-meter race, where the fastest men in the world lined up at the starting blocks in Barcelona, Spain. The network commentators began to tell the story of one of those runners, Derrick Redman, an athlete from Great Britain. He was called a "miracle boy" because he had endured twenty-two surgeries on his Achilles tendon prior to the race. It was a miracle he was even able to run, much less qualify for the Olympics. During this event, however, tragedy struck again. He suddenly grabbed his leg, pulled up short, and tumbled to the ground. He had pulled a hamstring and faced still another injury.

The commentators quickly announced that Redman was out of the race, and the cameras followed the rest of the runners to the tape. After identifying the winners, however, all attention returned to Derrick Redman, who was attempting to hoist himself back up and finish the race. He knew his country didn't send him all that way for him to merely start the race but to finish it. He began hobbling forward, wincing with each step. His face grimaced in agony as every step he took shot pain through his body.

Sitting in the stands, second row from the top was Jim Redman. He was not only Derrick's dad but his mentor. Jim felt compelled to get involved. He pushed his way past the huge crowd, climbed over the gate that separated the people from the track, and pushed his way past the two security guards beside that gate. Jim had prepared Derrick for this race, getting up early with him, running and cycling each day, and purchasing the Nikes and Reeboks. He was Derrick's biggest fan through the years, and this move was the only logical one for him.

The cameras quickly focused on this intruder, moving closer and closer to Derrick as he hobbled toward the finish line. Soon, he caught up with him. He gently put his hand on Derrick's shoulder. It must have been a familiar touch, because Derrick took only a few more steps, then twisted and turned, falling into the chest of his father. He was sobbing. The two men just held each other for a moment, as if no one was watching. Then, they exchanged words. I am certain Jim asked Derrick the question: Are you sure you want to finish this thing? Derrick nodded.

According to the newspaper articles the next day, Jim Redman then spoke some classic words to Derrick: "Son, we started this thing together. We're going to finish this thing together." He then put his arm around Derrick's shoulder, placed Derrick's arm around his shoulder, and they finished the race together.

I watched this scene with tears in my eyes, not expecting to observe such an act of love that day, to receive such a clear snapshot of someone investing their life in someone else. This image is what sons long for. This image is what dads long for. The crowd applauded more loudly for these two men as they crossed the finish line than they did for the medalists. Whether he knew it or not, Jim Redman gave the world a picture of a mentor, someone who says, "I'm going to make sure you finish your race well."

Ironically, four years earlier at the 1988 Olympics, we were given a negative illustration on mentoring. Four of the fastest men in the world were poised at the start of the 4 x 100-meter relay. Runner Carl Lewis was sure to win another gold medal. It was inconceivable that the United States team—each athlete a champion in his own right—could lose. Yet, as the final leg of the race approached, the unthinkable happened. The Americans dropped the baton. The race and any hopes of a gold medal were lost. All their potential was nullified because of a botched handoff.

This metaphor illustrates what happens far too often in homes across America. The baton gets dropped. One generation fails to pass on the resources to the next generation so that they can run their leg of the race. Many sons and daughters are stranded at the starting blocks without a baton.

Why does this happen? It certainly isn't a lack of desire to pass the baton of leadership. Perhaps it is the fear that we can't. When asked to see the future through a child's eyes, many parents express fear or concern. Most of them believe the best time to have been a child was between 1950 and 1990. The majority expects the future to be characterized by deteriorating moral conditions, new family stresses, and other personal tensions.[1]

Recent surveys concur that more than four out of five adults believe it is more difficult to raise children today than when their parents were raising them. Parenting has become so burdensome to many adults that they feel paralyzed by the weight of the decisions they must make. They are confronted by laws that restrict the autonomy of parents, by scientific research that has shown how improper parenting can create dysfunctional behavior in children, and by disputes over education and how to instill proper values in kids. In addition, there is pressure to make sure kids get all the extracurricular activities in after school. It is not surprising that a 1990 survey by NORC (National Organization for Raising Children) discovered that 85 percent of the respondents believe that "parents often feel uncertain about what is the right thing to do in raising their children." Our uncertainty increases as we raise the bar and attempt to raise our kids to be leaders. If there is one condition that makes parents uncomfortable, it is uncertainty.

CERTAINTY VERSUS CLARITY

My good friend and pastor, Andy Stanley, has an encouraging word for parents and leaders who struggle with the uncertainty that's always a part of leadership. Whether it is our workplace or our home, we'll encounter situations that make us uncertain. The answer is *not* to sit idly until we are certain. We might never act if we wait that long. The answer is to move forward in the direction we believe is right and to be clear. Clarity is much more important than certainty. As a parent, I may not know what is around the bend tomorrow—but I must be clear when I do speak and act. I may not have a lot to say on an issue, but when I speak, I must be clear.

Haven't you wondered why cult leaders such as Charles Manson, Jim Jones, or David Koresh persuaded young people to follow their leadership, even to the point of death? The answer is simple: In a world of confusion, they offered clarity.

In the words of the apostle Paul, we cannot blow an "uncertain trumpet." When I am unclear with my kids, I fail to model any leadership. Further, when we are unclear, our kids will turn to other voices who are clear. The clearest voice may be from MTV, a friend, a movie, a teacher, or an enemy at school, but the clear voice is the one they will tend to follow. As parents, we must learn to live with uncertainty, but we cannot be unclear. Be simple; be brief; be clear.

FOUR ROLES WE MUST FILL

Now that we have laid this foundation, there are four tangible roles we must play as we attempt to nurture the leader in our kids. These roles enable us to understand the keys to their heart and to mentor them well. These roles can be summarized in the following four word pictures.

1. The Host.

You already know what a good host does. If I were your friend and visited your house, what would you do to be a good host? You would probably invite me in, take my coat, ask me to sit down, and maybe offer me something to drink. You never read a book on it, but you already know how to be a good host.

This is a great picture for us with our kids. As a mentor in your home, you are to host the relationships and the conversations you have there.

You are not a guest. Guests expect someone else to take care of them. Guests respond. Hosts initiate. We are to host the primary relationships of our life, especially the ones with our children.

Good hosts take initiative with conversation, make others feel comfortable, create a safe environment to talk, and meet needs. Hosts are not so caught up in their own agenda that they fail to note others in the home. They are not playing "defense" but "offense." They look for opportunities to serve. There is no such thing as a good host who is passive.

While this is a simple metaphor, it is profound. Our greatest temptation when we get home is to get caught up in our own agenda. We are tired from a hectic day and want to relax or get busy doing necessary domestic chores. Instead, focus on assuming the role of the host in your home.

The Law of Connection

Dr. John C. Maxwell teaches the "laws of leadership." One such law, the "Law of Connection," reminds leaders that they must touch a heart before they ask for a hand. For example, before I can expect my kid to want to learn about leadership, I must lead him; before I can lead him, I must learn to connect with his heart. Only then will he reciprocate with a desire to learn.

There are simple rules for connecting. I've mentioned already we must find common ground to stand on. The root word for *communication* is the word "common." We must use the familiar to be a bridge to the unfamiliar. Although my world was, indeed, different than the one my kids are growing up in, I still talk to them about my memories of growing up. They love stories. In fact, at this point, my kids actually ask for stories about my childhood—and I can teach from those stories when I tell them. They're personal. They're interesting. They're helpful.

One mother decided to do this. She began telling her little girl what her childhood was like: "We used to skate outside on the pond. I had a swing made from a tire; it hung from a tree in our front yard. We rode our pony. We picked wild raspberries in the woods." The little girl was wide-eyed, taking this in. At last she said to her mom, "I sure wish I'd gotten to know you sooner!"

Hosting our kids may mean we have to change the way we "do family." Perhaps we limit TV or Internet time and learn to "unpack the day." Someone once said that with the appearance of the two-bathroom home, families forgot how to cooperate; with the two-car home, families forgot how to associate; and with the two-TV home, families forgot how to communicate.

When we play host to our children, we communicate that we accept them. Children need an adult to host them. It is part of the development of their self-worth. Authors Rick and Kathy Hicks asked 100,000 children between the ages of eight and fourteen what they wanted most in their parents, and published the results in *Boomers, Xers, and Other Strangers*. Note that most replies involved acceptance from an adult "host." These children want parents who:

- communicate their interest in me;

- express appreciation for each member of our family;

- structure their lives to spend time together;

- welcome my friends into our home;

- answer my questions;

- are committed to each other;

- deal with crisis in a positive way;

- are honest;

- correct kids when needed, but not in front of friends;

- don't argue in front of me;

- concentrate on strengths instead of weaknesses;

- and are consistent.[2]

Getting Your Kid to Talk

If you take this role of hosting seriously, your challenge will be to get your child to talk. Here are some ideas on how you might do this:

1. Start a project together. Do something that engages their mind and gets them to work cooperatively with you. See what comes up in your conversations.

2. Watch a good video together. Afterwards, talk about the characters they identified with. Discuss any leadership scenes in the movie. Was there anything to learn?

3. Read the editorials in the newspaper. Ask them for their opinions.

4. Write out questions and put them inside balloons. Have the family bat the balloons around. At a signal, have each member pop one and answer the question inside their balloon.

5. Read the comics together. Discuss the humor and the point of each comic strip.

6. Look at old photographs. Discuss whether your parents did a good job raising you.

7. Ask your child to teach you to do something they can do well that you can't do well.

8. Talk about current TV commercials. What methods did they use to persuade you?

2. The Doctor.

I'm sure you have visited a doctor's office. No doctor who was worth his or her salt would ever greet you, hand you a bottle of medicine immediately, and say, "I've just been to this fabulous conference on penicillin. I've got a sample of it right here. Why don't you try it? I'm sure you'll love it. You should have heard others share how much it has helped them!"

Why would a good doctor never do that? Because even though doctors are intelligent, have been to medical school, and may even suspect what is wrong with you before looking at your chart, they never give a prescription without first making a diagnosis! Regardless of their training and experience, they always take some time to look into your eyes and ears, examine your throat, listen to your heart, and tell you to cough.

Only after much poking and prodding will they draw a conclusion and give you a prescription.

I have a question for you. Have you learned to poke and prod? For years, parents have been guilty of dishing out prescriptions of advice to their kids without first poking and prodding them to make sure they're relevant. Often, parents never get connected, assuming that they have some experience in an area and don't need to communicate interest by asking questions. Many times parents give children an answer and send them on their way. You must take the time to ask all the necessary questions to draw proper conclusions. I know of a doctor who is in litigation right now because he failed to properly diagnose a patient. He didn't take the time to ask all the questions necessary to draw the proper conclusions. Both the doctor and the patient are paying for it. The takeaway is obvious. What if your kids could take you to court if you dished out prescriptions before making a diagnosis? Would you be in court right now?

As parents, we must get comfortable with poking and prodding our kids with good questions. We need to be patient. When I'm on the road and call home, I prepare two questions to ask my kids when I get them on the phone. When I mentor students outside of my family, I prepare a set of five questions to ask them when we meet. Why? Because I don't converse as naturally as I would like. I need to get ready to poke and prod. The questions aren't spectacular, and they may be as simple as:

- Did anything unusual happen at school today?

- Did you get to play with (your best friend)?

- What did your teacher think about your assignment?

- What kind of day was it today?

- Did you get a chance to help anyone?

- What was the best part about the day for you?

The point is not to get through all your questions but to get them talking comfortably and to communicate your interest in them. This deepens their sense of personal worth—they feel valuable to you—which builds a foundation for their leadership. Psychologists tell us that our self-worth is based on what we think the most important person in our lives thinks about us. For a while, you are the most important person in your child's life.

When young leaders fail to build this foundation of self-worth, they will sabotage their future or perform to gain acceptance until they burn out. Minimally, they will live with an insecure feeling regardless of how influential they become. In a recent interview pop star Madonna said: "My drive in life is from this horrible fear of being inadequate and mediocre. It's always pushing me and pushing me, because even though I've become somebody, I still have to prove that *I am somebody.* My struggle has never ended and it probably never will." What a tragic commentary, but so-o-o-o-o common in our society.

Tony Campolo told a story long ago that illustrates what I am trying to say.

Years ago, a young teacher learned the value of this foundation in kids. Miss Thompson had just begun to teach the third grade. In her first year, she had a troubled student named Teddy Stollard. He was sort of her initiation to the teaching profession. Teddy was rebellious, distracting to the other students, and always found ways to get attention. It didn't matter whether it was negative or positive. Miss Thompson responded with lots of time-outs and discipline. She put him in remedial groups, since he wasn't keeping up with the rest of the class. She could hardly wait for Christmas break.

On their last day before the break, the class celebrated a Christmas party. Some of the kids brought Miss Thompson a gift. Teddy brought two. When she opened his, they drew giggles from his classmates. The first was a string of pearls—half of them were missing. The second was a bottle of half used perfume. To prevent further disruption, Miss Thompson quieted the giggles by trying on the necklace and the perfume. She told Teddy how much she liked them and that she was proud to wear them.

When the bell rang, all the kids left, except for Teddy. He remained to say something to his teacher. It was their first serious conversation all year. "Miss Thompson," he mumbled. "I'm glad you like the pearls. Ummmm. You look just like my mom used to look." There was a pause. "And Miss Thompson. I'm glad you like the perfume, too. You smell just like my mom." Then, he walked out of the room.

Miss Thompson suddenly realized there was more to Teddy's story than she understood. She decided to check out Teddy's file in the school office. When she examined it, everything made sense. When Teddy was in kindergarten, his mother had gotten very sick. By the first grade she was bedridden. She had died while he was in second grade. Now, Teddy was trying to cope with life without mother. Miss Thompson hurt for Teddy and decided to change her approach. She determined to show special interest in Teddy and find out what made him tick. In short, she decided to "poke and prod" instead of just punishing him. She wanted to make sure her prescription was based on a proper diagnosis.

January was a transforming month. As she asked questions, and gave love to Teddy, he responded beautifully. His rebellion ceased. He wasn't a distraction anymore. In fact, by the end of the semester, he became a model student. He even helped Miss Thompson after class. When the school year ended, Teddy did his best to thank Miss Thompson for what she did.

Years went by and Miss Thompson taught many more third grade classes. She did her best to remember the lesson she learned from Teddy. It became easy about a decade later. Teddy wrote her a note:

Dear Miss Thompson,

I just wanted you to know, I graduate from high school today. I bet you thought I could never do that. Thank you for helping me through the third grade. You are the reason I made it this far.

Love,

Teddy Stollard

Needless to say, she kept the letter. Four years later, she got another one:

Dear Miss Thompson,

I just wanted to write and tell you I graduated from college today, second in my class. I bet you thought I could never do that. Thanks for helping me through the third grade. I would not have made it without you.

Love,

Teddy Stollard

Five years later, Miss Thompson got a third and final letter from Teddy:

Dear Miss Thompson,

I wanted to write you and tell you I am now Theodore Stollard, M.D. I graduated from medical school today, first in my class. I bet you thought I could never do that. I wanted to thank you again for making such a difference in my life, when I was nine years old. You are the reason I made it here.

One more thing, Miss Thompson. This summer, I am getting married. I wondered if you would be willing to come and sit where my mother would have sat in the ceremony. I can't think of anyone I would rather have sit there. Please write and tell me if you can.

Love,

Teddy Stollard

Miss Thompson did take part in Teddy's wedding. It was a milestone for her and a reminder of the difference someone can make when they decide to invest in, not just instruct a child.

3. The Counselor.

If you've ever been to see a counselor, you know they can teach us a valuable lesson. Good counselors always have something in common. They are active listeners. Once the client feels safe and begins to talk, they find excellent ways to communicate that they hear what is being said; that they understand; and that they are connecting with the client's thoughts.

They know they will earn the right to speak when they listen. They know that a person's favorite voice to hear is their own voice. They know that the number one emotional need of people today is the need to be understood.

We, too, must become active listeners. We must not only host conversations and ask leading questions, but we must find verbal and nonverbal ways to communicate that we "get it" when our kids talk to us. Leaders and parents who listen well elicit fierce loyalty from others. Sometimes this is all we need to do. Often our children don't want or need for us to give them an answer. They need an empathetic ear; they need to think out loud. They need understanding.

Katie was just seven years old when she taught her dad this lesson. One afternoon, Katie asked if she could play with her friend next door. Dad replied it would be fine as long as she was home by 6:00 P.M. Unfortunately, Katie was not home by 6:00 P.M. Dad grew a little upset when he had to call and ask that Katie be sent home.

When she got home a half-hour late, her dad said, "Didn't you hear me tell you to come home by 6:00?"

"Yes," she replied, "but my friend's doll broke."

Her dad mellowed a bit. "Oh, I see. And you stayed to help her fix it?"

"No," Katie whispered. "I stayed to help her cry."

Sometimes as we lead and mentor our children, they don't need us to "fix" anything. They need us to help them cry. They need someone to understand them and identify with where they are.

Here are some reminders for you to help you master your role as a counselor:

1. Timing is everything.
   Like adults, kids might be more responsive at certain times of the day. Be observant. Learn the best times to have heart-to-heart conversations.

2. Listen and talk with your eyes.
   When talking with your children (especially teens), look them in the

eye. This powerfully communicates that you really care about them and what they say. Intimacy doesn't diminish when we stop talking but when we *stop listening*.

3. Watch your body language.
    Tapping fingers and challenging glares send the message, "You're wasting my time." I have to watch this one with my daughter. She likes to share every detail of her day . . . some of which seem irrelevant to her story!

4. First understand, then worry about being understood.
    Your child will inevitably break the rules or do something to disappoint you. Before you jump all over your kid, find out why the rules were broken. You can always express your concerns after you have listened, but you may never have the opportunity to hear heartfelt expressions if you launch into a verbal assault.

5. Allow emotions to be expressed appropriately.
    Anger is a natural response for everyone, but it must be handled properly. Anger doesn't equal rebellion. Coach your kids, as emerging leaders, to voice their anger with honesty and self-control. Likewise, learn to control your own reactions.

6. Be willing to be unpopular.
    Teens will not like every decision you make. That's not your primary concern. Be consistent. Don't back down from tough decisions just because your kids won't like you for a while.

Learning the Keys to Their Hearts

Again, Dr. John C. Maxwell teaches us to listen in order to discover the keys to the hearts of others. As you poke and prod (like a good doctor) and then listen (like a good counselor), you will understand the keys to your child's heart. You have to ask the right questions and *listen* to their answers. You may already know them. What would you say are the answers to these questions: What do your children cry about? What do they sing about? What do they talk about? What do they dream about? How well do you listen to your kids? When do you listen to them?

4. The Tour Guide.

Have you ever taken a vacation where you had a tour guide lead you? My wife and I were in Hawaii years ago and toured one of the islands. Our tour guide must have missed his calling to be a nightclub comic! He kept telling us mindless jokes. After a while, I felt we weren't going to see what we wanted to see or get where we needed to go. I wanted to say to him: "Hey, the reason we hired you was not for conversation or jokes but to get us to our destination!"

Bingo. The reason a tour guide is such a vivid analogy for us as we mentor our kids in leadership is simple. Our job is not just to be their buddy or merely to have fun. Our job is to help get them to their destination; a place they may not have been able to arrive at on their own.

This does not mean we have all the answers or try to control our kids. It means we assume the responsibility to navigate for them. We must provide them with the tools they need to make their mark on the world. This is a delicate balance. When my generation was young, Dr. Benjamin Spock's book, *The Common Sense Book of Baby Care and Child Care*, revolutionized the way parents looked at rearing kids. He reacted to other books that profiled parenting as a regimented task. Many sources up to that point discouraged showing affection. Dr. Spock did families a service by encouraging parents to treat children as little people with needs, rather than soldiers in boot camp.[3]

Unfortunately, many parents took Dr. Spock's principles to an extreme, becoming overly permissive and withholding discipline. Many of these baby-boomer children grew up to be self-centered and undisciplined as adults. Tens of thousands protested the draft, took drugs, demonstrated on college campuses, participated in free sex, abused alcohol, and challenged the establishment in the '60s and '70s.

The solution, of course, is for us to strike a balance between extremes. We must mentor our kids in leadership with both love and discipline. We must encourage them to make their own way in this world, but we also must give them boundaries.

Some years ago, a Peruvian airliner crashed into the mountains shortly after takeoff in Peru. Why did such a tragedy happen? Just before takeoff, the plane had been washed and cleaned. During the process, masking tape had been used to cover the sensors of the plane that feed the information into the instruments. Unfortunately, the cleaners forgot to uncover the sensors and the instruments in the plane were conveying misinformation. The pilots were yelling in the cockpit that their instruments were not making any sense. There was no clear signal. The result was a tragic plane crash.

I just met a parent who illustrates my point. She has a nine-year-old son, who she believes is full of potential to be a leader. But, as she tries to help him, she fails to recognize the damage she does. Last week, her son was challenged to do something that would stretch his skills and confidence. Wanting to protect him, she made excuses in front of him as to why he couldn't fulfill the challenge. I am certain she meant well, but she was taking the wind right out of his sails. Putting him into a box, she removed his incentive to try something new. Unfortunately, her son lived up (or down) to her expectations.

Striking a Balance

As parents who want to see our kids grow into their leadership potential, we must strike the balance between *unchecked tyranny* and *uncritical tolerance.* Being a tour guide does not compel us to control our kids. We must get over this desire to control. It is ironic that baby boomers once took drugs when they were young to prompt impulses and to think outside the box. Today, they turn to drugs to suppress their kids' impulses and keep behavior inside the box. Nowadays, Dennis the Menace would be on Ritalin and Charlie Brown on Prozac! Control is king.

On the other hand, uncritical tolerance is not the answer either. While I understand the importance of tolerance in our society, tolerance is not the unthinking acceptance of all points of view as equally valid. Rather, it is practicing forbearance with those who are different and engaging in discussion as we pursue the truth. This is valid even with our kids.

I'm challenging you here to be a *tour guide*, not a *travel agent*. The difference is simple. A travel agent tells you where you can go, but a tour guide actually takes the journey with you. We cannot simply tell our kids to be good leaders; we must help them experience it. For instance, when my son or daughter doesn't understand a leadership principle or fails in some way, I must stop and consider what will best help them get it. I tell myself: Don't think *react*, think *result*. Instead of reacting to their failure or disobedience (which I am tempted to do), I try to think of what would help them grasp the truth in an unforgettable way. I ask these questions:

- Why are they not learning this important principle?
- What outcome do I wish to see happen in their life?
- How would this life change best take place?
- Where is a place this lesson could be taught?
- When could we participate in this learning experience?

When my daughter, Bethany, was five, my wife and I noticed she was developing a selfish attitude. She expected new toys from parents and grandparents on a regular basis. We wanted to teach her to have a grateful heart. That summer, we took her on a trip to Croatia with a team of students from our church. We fed the refugees who were living in campsites there. We gave the adults food for their families and the children toys. Bethany even gave away one of her own toys to a small girl who had nothing. The experience was both educational and entertaining. On our first day, she brought her Barbie doll to a refugee camp. When we spotted a small girl standing alone, I suggested Bethany give her the doll. My daughter hesitated. She wasn't ready to part with it. After lots of coaxing, I gave up and decided to go back to our campsite. At that point, Bethany agreed to give it away. But when we approached the girl, she hesitated again and began crying. It turned into a major event. Bethany did end up giving her doll away, but her last words were: "It's not fair! I had it first!" Bethany has never forgotten that life-changing trip, and we often refer to the lessons we learned there. Today, our family takes trips to Safehouse

Outreach in downtown Atlanta to feed the homeless. It is a constant reminder of how fortunate we are and of how we need to help those who are in need.

BE THE SALT OF THE EARTH

My wife and I have accepted the challenge to practice these four roles. We try to "salt" our children's lives by providing the roles of host, doctor, counselor, and tour guide for them. How about you? Be the "salt" that flavors and seasons life at home. When I take my kids on a date, I create environments for conversation. I keep a little acronym in mind. It spells the word: SALT.

> S—SAY ANYTHING. This is the role of a host who takes initiative.
>
> A—ASK QUESTIONS. This is the role of the doctor who pokes and prods.
>
> L—LISTEN WELL. This is the role of the counselor who actively absorbs.
>
> T—TRANSITION TO THE TRUTH. This is the role of the tour guide, who communicates key truths and gets the people to their destination.

"Daddy, how much do you make an hour?" With a timid voice and idolizing eyes, the little boy greeted his father as he returned home from work.

Greatly surprised, the dad gave his son a glaring look and said, "You're too young to know that. Besides, I'm tired. Don't bother me now."

"But, Daddy, just tell me, please! How much do you make?" the boy insisted. The father finally gave up and replied, "Twenty dollars an hour."

"Okay, Daddy. Could you loan me ten dollars?" the boy asked. Showing his restlessness, the father yelled, "So that was the reason you asked how much I earn? Be still and go to sleep." After it was dark, the father began reflecting on his impatience. He felt a bit guilty. *Maybe,* he thought, *my son wants to buy something.* To ease his mind, he went in to his son's room to see if he was still awake.

"Are you asleep?" he whispered.

"No," replied the boy, partially asleep. Then, his dad gave him a twenty-dollar bill and said, "Here's the money you asked me to loan you earlier."

"Thanks, Daddy!" he smiled. "Now, I have enough. Now, I have twenty dollars." When his father looked confused, he looked at his son as if to say: "What do you want to buy?"

"Daddy, could you sell me one hour of your time?"

I must constantly remind myself of the priority of practicing these roles with my kids. There is likely nothing I will do today that will be as important or have such a lasting impact.

Reflect and Respond

1. Would your child say you offer clear leadership?

2. How do you host your kids?

3. How do you communicate to your kids that you are listening?

PART 2

WHAT THEY NEED TO KNOW

5

PAINTING THE PRIMARY COLORS OF A LEADER IN YOUR KID

It is in developing others that we truly succed.
—HARVEY FIRESTONE

LEADERS HAVE A COMPASS IN THEIR HEADS AND A MAGNET IN THEIR HEARTS

JOURNAL ENTRY: MY MOM AND DAD KEEP talking about my potential. They say I am a leader. That scares me. Leadership is so complex. I could never do all the things a leader does. I just wish I could tell my parents. Part of me wants to live up to their expectations—but another part wants to sit back and just surf the Net. Right now, it sounds a lot easier to sit back and surf the Net.

This journal entry captures the mind and heart of most young people. They want to influence others with their lives, but most don't *feel* like a great leader.

One of the first movies to come out in the twenty-first century was *Pay It Forward.* It vividly depicts the world of the new millennial generation. In it a middle-school teacher challenges his social studies class to do one thing that would "change the world." One student, Trevor McKinney, takes him seriously. He rides his bike down to the dump and picks up a homeless man. After bringing him home for food and sleep, the poor man tries to thank him. Trevor tells him to just go out and help three other people in need. Then, those three are to be given the same instructions, and so on. That week in class, he proposes the idea to his classmates. He lays out a plan where they could literally change the world. By the time the movie is finished, this young boy has had an impact on millionaires and the impoverished, and a news reporter even does a story about him.

Trevor's real motive, however, is to try and fix his own world. His mother is single and in debt. She has a drinking problem. She has few healthy relationships with men. Trevor eventually brings together his teacher and his mom to create the family he has always wanted. Near the end of the movie, however, young Trevor is murdered while trying to help a classmate fend off a bully. The closing scene depicts a candlelight vigil of hundreds outside of his house, communicating the impact the young boy had on so many. He had, in fact, changed his world.

I was so captivated by this movie that I spent some time analyzing what was so arresting about its story. My observations from the movie all illustrate the world of this new group of kids growing up right today:

1. The world they live in is broken.

2. They want to fix their world.

3. They long for family.

4. They don't understand all the fear in others.

5. They will pay a price to do what is right.

6. They will believe adults who tell them they can change their world.

Number six distinguishes millennials from previous generations. Historically, most teens simply want to fit in with their friends and be accepted. *Newsweek* magazine printed the results of a poll of thirteen- to nineteen-year-olds in May 2000. They asked teens, "If you had to choose between fitting in with friends or becoming outstanding in some way, which would you choose?" Only 26 percent said "fitting in," yet seven out of ten said they would choose to do something outstanding.[1]

BUILDING THEM INTO LEADERS

So, how do we help them change their world? How do we foster the leadership gifts in them? The subject of leadership can be overwhelming, especially to a kid. When they see an adult leader, it all seems so complex. They may have heard it involves things like vision, planning, communication, budgets, empowerment, delegation, downsizing, and training. My kids don't know the meaning of some of those words, much less how to do them. So, how do we build them into leaders?

I think we must begin by determining what qualities they need to possess to become a leader. What is the essence of a healthy leader? What is negotiable and what is essential? What are the common qualities that great leaders possess that enable them to influence others and bring about change?

THE PRIMARY COLORS

When I was in college, I took an art history class. One afternoon, my professor brought prints of several masterpiece paintings to class. He took the entire period to hold each one up and detail how unique it was. After each one, though, he would look us in the eye and say, "Now just think. This masterpiece started with just a few primary colors." We must have looked at twenty paintings during that class—and he would follow each one with the same remark. The phrase rang in my ear: "Each painting started with just a few primary colors."

Later, as I was thinking about my kids, I related that phrase to them. Like those paintings, every one of our children is a masterpiece; each one is unique and priceless. And each of them will lead others uniquely.

Like the paintings, however, they will always have a few primary colors inside, if they are to become healthy, effective leaders. Just as a painter begins with a palette of red, yellow, blue, and white, every leader must have four primary colors inside of them if they are to influence others in a masterful way. Your child is wired uniquely, but you can help him or her immensely if you instill these four fundamentals:

Four Primary Colors of a Leader
Character + Perspective + Courage + Favor =
Healthy, Effective Leadership

Let's talk about these primary concepts. In fact, let me give you a plan to talk about and practice these primary colors with your kids, so you both can develop them in your life.

1. Character.

Character enables a leader to do what is right, even when it is difficult.

In the 1990s, character became a front-burner item in the minds of Americans. The big debate during the Clinton scandals was: Does character count? Can someone be a good leader without it? The answer of course is yes . . . but only for a short while. If your child becomes a strategic thinker and a charismatic influence but fails to develop character, he eventually will sabotage his leadership. Ability may get them to the top, but it takes character to keep them there.

Character is the foundation on which the leader's life is built. Why? Leadership operates on the basis of trust. My wife, Pam, and I constantly talk to our kids about being trustworthy. If they can't be trusted, they won't be followed. Leadership development must begin with character development. You can have character and not be a great leader, but you can't be a great leader without character. J. R. Miller wrote: "The only thing that walks back from the tomb with the mourners and refuses to be buried, is the character of a man. What a man is—survives him. It cannot be buried."

Many school districts nationwide have introduced character training into their curriculum. Parents and educators have finally agreed that good character is a prerequisite to good conduct. Consider *The Book of Virtues*, William Bennett's landmark book. Midlife boomers agree children need to be taught his ten values—self-discipline, compassion, responsibility, friendship, work, courage, perseverance, honesty, loyalty, and faith.[2]

At a country fair a few years ago, a man encountered a little girl with a huge mass of cotton candy on a paper cone. He asked, "How can a little girl like you eat all of that cotton candy?"

"Well you see, Mister," she answered, "I'm really much bigger on the inside than I am on the outside."

That's exactly the kind of kids I want to raise! I want them to be big on the inside. Good character is to be praised more than outstanding talent. Most talents are, to some extent, a gift. Good character, by contrast, is not given to us, or our kids. We all must build it piece by piece—by thought, choice, courage, and determination.

An Era of Untruths Sets a Bad Example

In the early days of American history, Henry Clay lobbied for some unpopular legislation he believed was right for America. A friend told him that his bill would ruin his chance to become president. Henry Clay responded, "I would rather be right than president."

Oh, could we use those words today. In August 1998, we learned from the political arena to say whatever you need to say to stay in office. Lie if you have to, because later you can redefine what your words meant; truth is relative. When you're finally forced to confess to failure, you don't have to apologize. Just tell the people it is time to move on. After all, the economy is good.

High school students in a 1996 survey considered moral decline the biggest problem facing America, as well as the number one issue facing teenagers, according to Thomas Harvey in *Mission America*. Sadly, more than three-fourths of the students admitted to cheating.[3] Are students learning to accept lying by imitating what they see from the current adult generation?

This calls to mind the story of a middle-school teacher, who criticized the lifestyle of her class. She said, "I don't like the destructive toys, the violent video games, or the weird books your generation reads!" One student thought for a moment, then asked her, "Whose generation made those toys, games, and books?" If we're going to turn our kids' generation around, we'll have to fix the damage *our* generation has done. We cannot afford to enter this new century and make the same mistakes as we did in the last one.

Summing Up the Issue

Work with your child to build character in their life, focusing on the development of:

1. personal discipline

2. personal security and identity

3. personal convictions, values, and ethics

Steps Your Child Can Take to Develop Character

1. Have them discipline themselves to do two things they don't like *every week.*

2. Help them set one goal and focus on one to three steps they can take toward it.

3. Explain the "whys" behind your rules and instructions to them.

4. Have them interview a leader who has integrity: How did they build character into their life?

5. Discuss their motives with them. Ask them why they do what they do.

6. Ask them to write in a journal the kind of person they want to be as an adult.

7. Have them write out promises they've made. Hold them accountable to take responsibility for all their actions and emotions.

But now, a personal question. Are you a person of character? Do your children see character reflected in your life? In a court of law, would your wife, husband, child, or close friend say of you: "He/she would never lie"? These foundational principles begin with us, don't they?

2. Perspective.

Perspective enables a leader to see and understand what must happen to reach a goal.

A second primary color every good leader must develop is perspective. If your child is to consistently influence others, they must feed their minds. You've likely heard the phrase: Leaders are readers. I'll take it a step further: Leaders are feeders. They feed themselves first, and then naturally feed others with insights necessary to reach goals. Perspective distinguishes leaders from followers. Anyone can possess character. Leaders, however, think differently than followers do. Do you remember the difference between a thermostat and a thermometer? Leaders see before others do and see beyond what others do. They often see bigger than others do. One of my doctoral professors, Bobby Clinton, said: "The primary difference between a follower and a leader is perspective. The primary difference between a leader and an effective leader is better perspective." I am not suggesting your child must be brilliant. They must simply develop competence in some area.

As parents, we must help our kids construct strong character so that they will have the infrastructure in place to hold them up as they pursue their life plans. Then, we must help them think through their perspective on three key issues:

1. Their vision: What is it they want to accomplish in life?
   Example: "I want to help underprivileged kids find hope."

2. Their plans: What is their strategy to fulfill their vision?
   Example: "I want to be a teacher."

3. Their activities: What will they do to work their strategy?
   Example: "I will go to college and perform urban community service."

How important is it for kids to know what they want and where they're going? A study of graduates at one Harvard class thirty years later says it all. Eighty percent had no specific goals, 15 percent had ones they only thought about occasionally, and 5 percent had specific written goals (dreams with deadlines). Measured by net assets, the 5 percent had not only surpassed the goals they wrote down for themselves, but, as a group, had more net worth than the other 95 percent combined![4]

Vision is a powerful tool. Every great leader is motivated by a vision, regardless of whether they are young or old. Tiger Woods and Bill Gates captured their life-vision in high school. Some kids seem to get it even younger. Dennis Vilmer, from Grove, Oklahoma, was six when he had a vision to write a book. As a six-year-old he wrote and illustrated the book, *Joshua Disobeys*, and won a national contest in 1987. The 1973 thriller, *Lex the Wonderdog*, was written, produced, and directed by Sydney Ling, when he was just thirteen years old. It was a feature-length film. Laura Sweeting, from England, had a vision to be the youngest U.N. Goodwill ambassador ever. On June 9, 2000, she reached her goal, at age sixteen. John Payton was a teenager when he set a goal to become a judge. He took office as justice of the peace in Plano, Texas, in 1991. He was just eighteen years old.

Summing Up the Issue

To develop perspective, ask your children to focus on:

1. Reflecting on and interpreting the needs of the world around them.

2. Capturing a suitable vision for them to pursue.

3. Planning a strategy to solve problems, meet needs, and involve others.

Steps Your Child Can Take to Develop Perspective

1. Watch the news together. Select one crisis and answer the question: If I was in charge of this what would I do? List solution-steps they could take.

2. Groom the optimist in them. Have them read and listen to positive books and tapes. Feed them with big ideas from great people.

3. Have them write out their dreams. Then, have them list their skills and talents. Do any match? Ask them what they would do if they had no fear of failure.

4. Go with them to interview a visionary leader. Ask that leader how they think about problems. How do they perceive opportunities?

5. Discuss current events each week. Ask them to identify one burden or problem they see around them. List what could be done to address it.

6. Have them post photos, pictures, quotes, or scriptures that represent their goals and dreams, and remind them of what they could do if they tried.

7. Give them envelopes with their allowance. Let them distribute where their money will go each week. Discuss their decision-making process with them.

I have another personal question for you. Do your kids see you as a person with vision? Will they learn to plan a strategy from you? When they leave home one day, will they know how to come up with a life plan because they have watched you do it?

3. Courage.

Courage enables the leader to initiate a plan and to risk stepping out toward the goal.

Character is the infrastructure that holds a leader up when the winds of adversity are blowing. Perspective provides the vision a leader needs to make a difference. But without courage, the leader may still lack action. There is nothing more common in America than people with great ideas who do nothing about them. Only when a person exhibits courage do they act on ideas.

My dad demonstrated courage throughout the years when I was growing up. I can recall many times he would stand for what was right, whether it was a family rule, a spiritual conviction in church, or a political belief he held. When I was in high school, he came to a point where he wanted to prove to himself that his income wasn't running his life. He resigned his executive position at a prestigious company and went into business for himself with his brother. We moved across the country and started over, when he was forty-six years old. More than once, I have reflected on the impact of his courage and how it has affected my attitudes toward my family and my workplace.

Our kids must understand that the only measure of what we believe is what we *do*. If you want to know what people believe, don't read what they write; don't ask what they think; just observe what they do. Our lives shrink or expand in proportion to our courage. Consider these . . .

- Courage is contagious. When your child has it, it rubs off on others.

- Courage means initiating and doing what they are afraid of doing. Courage doesn't imply the absence of fear. Courage means they do it anyway.

- Courage is the power to let go of the familiar. It means trying new things.

- Courage is vision in action. It moves your child to step out toward their ideas.

- Courage means taking a risk and doing what is essential to make a difference.

When I surveyed students on these four primary colors of leadership, courage was the number one quality students felt they lacked. It's easier to play it safe. To stay with the familiar. It is human to choose the comfort zone over the end zone. But our kids will never get anywhere worthwhile without taking some risks. They must overcome their fears. During adolescence they naturally struggle with self-esteem issues and with their emotional security. Kids avoid failure like the plague, because it reflects personal inadequacy. They must establish their self-esteem. They must settle any security issues. They must be OK with failure. Failure isn't final unless they quit.

- Michael Jordan got cut from his high school basketball team his freshman year.

- Walt Disney was fired by a newspaper because they thought he "had no good ideas."

- Albert Einstein couldn't speak until he was four years old. He didn't read until he was seven.

- According to Beethoven's music teacher, "As a composer, [Beethoven] is hopeless."

- His teachers said as a boy Thomas Edison was so stupid he'd never learn anything.

- Missile and satellite expert Dr. Wernher Von Braun flunked math in his early teens.

- An expert said of famous football coach Vince Lombardi: "He possesses minimal football knowledge. Lacks motivation."

- Sir Isaac Newton finished next to the lowest in his class and failed in geometry.

- Eighteen publishers rejected Richard Bach's story, *Jonathan Livingston Seagull.* Macmillan finally published it, and by 1975, it sold more than 7 million copies in the U.S.

- After Fred Astaire's first screen test, the MGM director said: "Can't act. Slightly bald. Can dance a little." (Astaire hung that memo in his Beverly Hills home!)

Ask your child this question: What might have happened if these individuals lacked courage to go on? What would have happened had they run from their failure and quit? I have laughed several times at the story of General George Steadman. This Civil War officer apparently had a premonition as to how the battle of Bull Run was going to turn out, so he addressed his Confederate troops just before the battle. "Gentlemen," he said, "I want you to fight vigorously and then run away. As I am a bit lame, I am going to begin running now."

It is always easier to coach someone else into courage than to display it yourself. Two small boys walked into the dentist's office. One of them said bravely, "I want a tooth taken out and I don't want any gas, and I don't want it deadened because we're in a hurry!" The dentist was impressed. He said, "You're quite a brave young man. Which tooth is it?" The boy turned to his smaller friend and said, "Show him your tooth, Tommy."

What we have to remember is that leaders have to show the way. Action is essential. The armchair quarterback always sounds so convincing—but does nothing from his easy chair! Courage is simple only in theory.

Let me encourage you not only to talk about courage with your children, but to do something together that requires you both to demonstrate some courage. Winston Churchill wrote, "Courage is the first of all human qualities because it is the one which guarantees all the others."

Summing Up the Issues
Affirm the ability of your children to:

1. Make and keep commitments.

2. Take a stand and take risks.

3. Show the tenacity to lobby for a cause.

Steps Your Child Can Take to Develop Courage
1. Ask them to attempt something every week that is bigger than they are. Something that is very important and almost impossible . . . to them. Discuss these adventures.

2. Hold each other accountable on commitments and decisions you both have made.

3. Have them try this assignment: Give an all-out commitment to a good

habit for a set time. Talk about the results. What did they choose to do? How did they do?

4. Have them interview a courageous person. What gives them their courage?

5. Talk about what they fear the most. What would happen if they attacked that fear?

6. See a movie in which a character exhibits courage. Discuss why they acted bravely. What gave them the capacity to be bold, to try something new, to be different?

7. Ask them to reflect on something they have procrastinated in doing. Challenge them to be a decision maker in that area. Ask them to take one responsible step to beat it.

Here are two more personal questions for you. Do you model courage in your home? Do your kids learn fear and caution or courage and initiative when they watch you?

4. Favor.

Favor enables the leader to attract and empower others to join them in the cause.

Character helps the leader do what's right in difficult times. Perspective helps the leader choose a direction and navigate the steps. Courage helps the leader to begin to take that journey, even if no one goes with him at first. But with only these three qualities—we travel alone. We still haven't taken anyone else with us yet. Favor is the quality that enables a leader to connect with others and empower them to play a position on the team.

Just as trade skills can be learned, people skills can be developed as well. Some kids possess relationship skills more naturally than others because dealing with people comes easier to certain temperaments. However, I am an introvert who has learned people skills. My mother taught me the art of active listening and how to love everyone, regardless of their differences. She embraces everyone who comes into her life.

I believe before our kids learn to lead people, they must learn to love people. Having learned the basic people skills from my mom, I'm now working with my kids on the four word pictures in Chapter Four. They're learning how they can be a host, a doctor, a counselor, and a tour guide.

People skills work in this order—initiative, inquiry, interest, and influence. I can't tell you how proud it makes me to see my son, Jonathan, practicing these skills as an eight-year-old. Last week, I visited his school to have lunch with him. I discovered he has reached out to two new students in his class. He introduced me to them, asked them questions, made eye contact with them as he listened—and I noticed many of the kids wanted to sit next to him at lunch!

People skills are a leader's most important asset. For years, businesses have said that success is made up of 13 percent product knowledge and 87 percent people knowledge. Henry Ford once said, "You can burn up my buildings and take away my money—but give me my people, and I will build the business right back again." If we can mentor our kids in people skills, we will give them a head start on the leadership journey.

Advanced People Skills

As they get older, your children will need greater mentoring in these people skills. The quality of "favor" must grow beyond just being nice. In high school and college, they should be introduced to "The Big Five." As your child becomes a teen, talk with them about growing in these five areas:

1. Communication: Leaders must be able to listen and share ideas convincingly.

2. Motivation: Leaders must mobilize others to act and to benefit themselves and the organization.

3. Delegation: Leaders must spot gifts in others and share both authority and responsibility.

4. Confrontation: Leaders must have the backbone to resolve relationship differences.

5. Reproduction: Leaders must be able to equip and develop a team of people to accomplish a goal.

Summing Up the Issues

Work with your child to develop these abilities:

1. Learn to value people and spot their gifts.

2. Build personal charisma.

3. Develop skills in the Big Five: communication, motivation, delegation, confrontation, and reproduction.

Steps Your Child Can Take to Develop Favor

1. Teach them the four word pictures: host, doctor, counselor, and tour guide. Help them to host the conversations and relationships they engage in.

2. Help them focus on one to three people in their life this week. Work with them to become "others-centered," focusing on their needs more than personal needs.

3. Work with them to become a "good finder." Each time they meet someone, help them find one good quality in them and compliment it.

4. Train them to be a resource person. When they see a need, talk it over with them. Then, ask if they could meet that need through encouragement, a book, a gift, etc.

5. Go with them to interview a leader who is a "people person." How did they develop their charisma? What motivates them to serve others?

6. Pay your child to read and discuss with you *How to Win Friends and Influence People,* by Norman Vincent Peale, or *You Can Be a People Person,* by Dr. John C. Maxwell.

7. Discuss the strengths of three to five friends they know. Next, imagine a specific project that would require a team to pull it off and ask your kid to pretend to be in charge of the project. How could their friends' strengths be used on a team to reach the goal?

Do your relationships at home prepare your kids for positive relationships outside your home? Do they learn to host people, ask questions, listen, and invite others to participate in groups?

WRAPPING IT UP

Let me close by stating the obvious. The best way to build the primary colors of a leader in your child is to model them yourself. Children do what children see. I encourage you to grow in these four areas together. When Woodrow Wilson was president of Princeton University, he spoke these words to a parents' group one afternoon:

> I get many letters from you parents about your children. You want to know why we people up here at Princeton can't make more out of them and do more for them. Let me tell you the reason we can't. It may shock you just a little, but I am not trying to be rude. The reason is that they are your sons, reared in your homes, blood of your blood, bone of your bone. They have absorbed the ideals of your homes. You have formed and fashioned them. They are your sons. In those malleable, moldable years of their lives you have forever left your imprint upon them.[5]

Reflect and Respond

1. Discuss the four primary colors of a leader with your child. Where are they strong? Where are they weak?

2. Where do they lead most naturally? Why?

3. What is one step they can take to grow in their leadership?

6

THE NATURAL LEADER VERSUS THE LEARNED LEADER

There is more in us than we know. If we can be made to see it, perhaps,
for the rest of our lives, we will be unwilling to settle for less.
—KURT HAHN, FOUNDER OF OUTWARD BOUND, 1886–1974

JOURNAL ENTRY: MY MOM AND DAD ARE pushing me to be something I'm not. I'm going to have to tell them I am just not a natural-born leader. I'm different. I don't feel like a leader. I'm not smart or outgoing. I'm afraid I will fail, and then I would disappoint my parents.

Sir Humphry Davy was a distinguished chemist during the nineteenth century. When he was asked late in his life what he considered to be his greatest discovery, he replied, "Michael Faraday."

Davy had discovered Faraday, the ignorant son of a blacksmith, taking notes at his lectures and longing to study science seriously. As Davy began to teach him, he found a brilliant mind that promised to eclipse even his own achievements. He knew that no discovery of his own could possibly compare with the many discoveries Faraday would make during his career. He saw the gold inside the young man.

He also knew that Faraday would never reach his potential without some help. Faraday was starting with some significant cultural and social disadvantages. All young Faraday had was a hungry mind. Davy began to invest more in this young "life" than he did in his laboratory—and the world has benefited ever since. Faraday became the famous chemist and physicist who discovered electromagnetic induction.

Like most parents, I dream of my kids doing something significant with their lives. I see gifts in them just like Humphry Davy saw in Michael Faraday. Each night I pray that God would give them more influence than their parents have had. Both of my kids have heard me pray and have asked, "Dad, why do you pray that way?"

I always answer them honestly. I tell them I see potential in them, and I don't want them to fall short of it. I can tell they don't understand because they don't see their potential as clearly as I do. They usually smile patronizingly, roll over, and go to sleep.

I know I am biased. Most parents are. We think our kids are something special from the moment we spot them. From the beginning, I wanted them to get involved with the activities I did as a kid. Early on, I began paying my kids to read books about great leaders, just to whet their appetite. My daughter read about Billy Graham, Corrie Ten Boom, and Abraham Lincoln this past year. We take time to discuss the books when she's done, or she writes a report on them. I'm sure she thinks she's just getting rich. I think she's getting rich in more ways than one!

STRIKING A BALANCE

I have to be cautious, though. As a parent I am very aware of the danger I can create if I am not careful. It is very easy to fail to find balance between the two extremes:

- **Control:** Forcing our children to become who we want them to become, instead of who they are. Leadership can become a drive parents have that their kids don't share. We parents push our kids into new challenges, sometimes against their will. Kids become victims and reactors to their parents' agenda. Children either fight it (and resent it now) or flow with it to appease Mom and Dad (and resent it later).

- **Compliance:** Fearing we might manipulate them, parents back off and fail to stretch them in the areas of their potential and gifts. The kids never get coached to make a difference. The home is a place of acceptance, but abilities go untapped. Everything is just fine the way it is. Children learn to go along with the crowd to fit in. They miss their potential and resent it.

I know many parents trying to strike the balance between these two extremes. Out of sheer excitement, they push their kids into soccer, Cub Scouts, youth groups, dance classes, piano lessons, Girl Scouts, and Little League. Then, they begin to feel they've pushed them too much, and back off completely, allowing them to become couch potatoes in front of a video game, movie, or computer program. This pendulum swings back and forth throughout the first fifteen years of their life, often due to the parents not knowing the difference between coaching and controlling.

What If My Child Isn't a Natural Leader?

Some kids naturally move into leadership roles and feel comfortable. Others shy away from them due to the strong personalities of classmates or peers. Both types need to be taught leadership appropriately. However, they need a discerning adult who can strike the balance between control and compliance. When it comes to leadership development, they don't need pushing or pampering—they just need permission.

If you are a parent with multiple children, you've already discovered how different they can be. Reared in the same home, with the same values, rules, diet (well, almost the same diet!), and parental genes, they can be as different as night and day. Some temperaments lend themselves to leadership more than others. Outgoing personalities seem to be natural leaders, while introverted personalities seem to be followers. Let me say right up front—this is a misperception. Some of my favorite leaders are introverted people. They are energized by time alone rather than by time with people, yet they are able to lead more effectively than some outgoing personalities I know!

There are two big questions parents and children must answer as they consider their leadership potential:

1. Can he? (Does my child have the abilities to lead?)

2. Will he? (Does my child aspire to lead?)

You must continually return to questions of ability and aspiration as your children mature. You must be honest and realistic about your answers. When you are, you will find that any temperament can be a leader. You will also find that all the stereotypes of leaders you've had in the past don't really matter.

MYTHS ABOUT LEADERSHIP

When we buy into myths, we are prevented from becoming all we were meant to be. Let's talk about some of the most common myths about leadership. I want to encourage you and your child with this list. In fact, I suggest you take some time and talk about them with your sons and daughters.

Myth One: Leaders Are Born, Not Made.

People have believed this for years. Our common vocabulary even lends itself to this myth: "the born leader." We observe certain personalities that are predisposed to taking charge or enjoying people, and we assume they must be able to lead others well. Several leadership books have been written over the last century disproving the idea that leaders are born with endowed qualities that make them superior to others. In fact, current research now shows that leadership is learned and based on context or situation. There is hope for everyone! I believe leadership can and must be learned by all. Research sponsored by the Kellogg Foundation concludes: "The capacity to lead is rooted in virtually any individual . . . leadership is no longer the province of the few, the privileged, or even the merely ambitious. Every student has the potential to be an effective leader."[1]

Myth Two: My Child Just Isn't Cut Out to Be a Leader.

This misconception comes from stereotypes we have about what leaders ought to look like. When we look at our own children and see they don't fit the stereotypes we have about what leaders ought to look like, we assume they must not be leaders. This is a tragedy. While I do believe some children are more comfortable taking charge than others are, I believe leadership can and must be learned. For instance, even personalities that have a bent toward "taking charge" must still learn people skills. Leadership development is a lifelong education for everyone.

All people have the capacity to influence others. They naturally become leaders when they find their purpose and live the life they were meant to live. Your children shouldn't have to force anything as they grow into a leader. They must mature into the people they really are. Once they zero in on a purpose that matches their gifts, then they can develop the skills that will improve their leadership ability.

I've already mentioned Dr. John C. Maxwell, author of the best-selling *The 21 Irrefutable Laws of Leadership*. He gives us a handle on what to expect from those who don't seem like natural leaders. He says that everyone has some leadership ability. If we were to measure it on a scale of one to ten, your child may only be a three. Realistically, they may never be a ten. However, because leadership can be learned, when they find their niche in life, and learn some leadership principles, they may be able to grow from a three to a six. In doing so, they may not be a CEO of a corporation, but they just doubled their leadership ability! The key is this: your role as a leadership mentor is to help them reach *their* potential, not *your* expectations.

Myth Three: Leadership Means Being in Control and Having Power.

This has always been a myth, but our society is just now recognizing it as such. No leader, however powerful, is ever in control. They may be responsible for their organization. They may be in charge, but they are not in control. Control is a myth. We must be sure not to pass it on to our kids. The leadership paradox is this: the harder a leader tries to control a group, the less control he or she has. Effective leaders don't make control or power their goal. They enter situations as students and teachers.

Leadership is not about having power, either. Good leaders are *servants* first, not *leaders* first. Their goal is not to gain power but to serve others. Their ambition is not to control but to be helpful. They see leadership as the best way to serve people. We must teach our children the servant-leadership model. Do you remember the movie *Big*, starring Tom Hanks? In this movie, a twelve-year-old boy wakes up one morning looking like a thirty-year-old. On the outside he's thirty, but on the inside, he's still a kid. He gets a job with a toy manufacturer and is quickly promoted to vice president. He is working in his gift area: toys. To the amazement of his colleagues, he is praised for his leadership. His is an unlikely style that has nothing to do with dominance or power. His goal is simply to be himself—honest, playful, and asker of dumb questions. But by just being himself, he leads. Others in the company crunch numbers and jockey for position. He just brings himself to the job and creative things happen. He simply wants to help kids have fun playing with toys.

Myth Four: Leaders Have a Certain Temperament.

Major universities that study leadership formally used to say that if you were going to be an effective leader, you must have a driven, charismatic, Type A personality. Today, they say there is more than one right way to lead, and more than one right leadership personality. Your child does not have to be a dynamo to be an effective leader, nor do they have to fundamentally change who they are to lead. Instead, they must be themselves, develop the four primary colors of a leader, and find a suitable context in which to serve.

Your key as a parent will be to work with your child in an appropriate manner. John Gray has written *Children Are from Heaven*, in which he talks about working with children based on their personalities and "wiring." Some parents think it is right to treat their children exactly alike. They call it fair. But it isn't fair at all. We must treat kids based on who *they* are, not who *we* are. If we treat them alike, one temperament will fare well, and a different one will not. Dr. Gray tells kids that it's OK to be different, to have bad days, to feel negative emotions, to make mistakes. These things do not eliminate a child from being a leader.

In *Strong-Willed Child or Dreamer?*[2] authors Spears and Braund tell us there are three kinds of children: the drivers, the diplomats, and the dreamers.

1. Drivers are strong-willed. They need to be handled firmly and directly. Parents should communicate in black-and-white terms.

2. Diplomats are compliant, cautious. They need to be handled gently and warmly. They want to please parents. Parents should communicate by requesting cooperation.

3. Dreamers are creative, sensitive. They need to be handled sensitively and intuitively. Parents should give them creative options whenever possible.

Flexibility is the key. If you had a greenhouse, you wouldn't tell the tropical plants, "I don't like humidity, so you can just adjust to a little less water!" If you acted that way, your plants would die. The fact is, no child can bend too far from their God-given personality without breaking. A dreamer child may seem like a rebel at times, but that's not necessarily true. Their stubbornness isn't always due to a rebellious spirit; they just think outside the box. Some don't even have a box! Creativity and relationships speak to them most clearly.

Many kids are somewhere in between these three types. They could be called relaters, doers, and creators. They are a hybrid of other styles. The good news is that all three have positive leadership qualities! Whether your child is a relater, a doer, or a creator—all three styles contribute to their leadership potential.

Myth Five: Leadership Is Merely About Behavior and Position.

Wrong. Leadership is not merely something people "do." Authentic leadership reflects who we are, not just what we do. Your child should become the person they were born to be, and the rest will take care of itself. The fact is, genuine leadership is shared by the one in charge. The leader empowers others by distributing the leadership to them.

Our understanding of leadership has evolved over the last fifty years. Consider these changes:

1. **The Military Commander.** Fifty years ago, most looked at leadership as a military-style, "top-down" position. Presidents Dwight D. Eisenhower and John F. Kennedy both had military backgrounds. Good leadership meant strength at the top. The people were to follow and submit.

2. **The CEO.** In the 1970s, we began to expect leaders to share vision with their people. Staff would, in turn, be moved by this vision. This was a better model, since it moved from blind submission to the CEO leader, but it was still top-down in nature.

3. **The Coach.** By the late 1980s, we began to talk about teams and coaches playing together in order to win. The leader (the "one with the answers") became a broker of the talent and resources of the team. This was more participatory but was still top-down in nature.

4. **The Poet and the Gardener.** As the twenty-first century dawns, the new generation doesn't assume the leader has all the answers. Instead, the leader pulls together a team or inner circle. Then, as they share common goals and methods the leader becomes a poet and puts words to what the team is saying. Think about a poet you enjoy reading. What makes them good? They give language to feelings you already have. Poet leaders don't pretend to think up all the answers—and the pressure is off of them to have to.

   Leader-gardeners are people developers. The work of a gardener is to cultivate the soil, pull the weeds, and create an environment where plants can grow. In this new day we are in, leaders are people developers. Their job is to grow and resource staff to become all they can be.

True leaders empower others and share leadership! They distribute their leadership, based on the strengths the other team members bring to the table. Leadership has grown into something every child can aspire to.

I have watched all kinds of personalities and styles succeed on school campuses. Any child, including yours, can be a good leader.

So, What Do Leaders Do?

Let me shift gears from the myths to the truth. What is it that leaders do? If your child can learn leadership, and doesn't have to fundamentally change their personality, what kinds of skills or activities should they focus on to become authentic leaders? We can boil it down to these five:

1. They Perceive a Need.

True leadership doesn't begin with a position. It begins when a person perceives a need and feels they could and should do something about it. They get burdened over it, then somehow catch a vision for what could be done about that need. Consider Mother Teresa, a school teacher in Calcutta, who looked out the window of her safe classroom and saw impoverished people dying on the streets. She left her teaching position and began caring for the poor, without any encouragement or funding. She never sought a leadership position; she became a leader when she perceived a need.

I often talk to my kids about the needs in their world. I listen to their perceptions. Sometimes the needs are big, sometimes small. At some point, a need will arise that will match their personality and tug at their heart.

2. They Possess a Gift.

Leaders possess a gift that enables them to address a need. They have a primary ability that helps them choose the method for how they can meet that need. Consider Martin Luther King Jr. Segregation and racial prejudice were his burdens. Humans' rights were being violated. He stepped forward and began using his gift: words. He cast a vision to his generation. He stood on the steps of the Lincoln Memorial in 1963 and gave the most famous speech of the twentieth century: "I Have a Dream." The next year, the Civil Rights Act was passed in Washington, D.C.

I have many discussions about what my kids enjoy doing and the areas in which they feel they have some talent. My wife and I then attempt to place them in opportunities where they can develop those gifts. They are experimenting with drama, music, writing, singing, sports, and so on. It is all part of the discovery process, and we help them choose activities wisely.

3. They Parade a Passion.

All genuine leaders parade their passion. When an outward need and an inward gift match, the leader becomes consumed with a passion, shares it with others, and entices people to join them. Consider Winston Churchill, whose passion was the survival of the free world. When Adolf Hitler and the Third Reich began posing a threat to Europe, Churchill discerned the danger and cried out against it. Britain listened and made him prime minister. He paraded his passion until other nations, including the United States, finally joined him.

I am paying close attention to the interests of my children, since passion generally begins with interests. No doubt, my kids will be drawn to fads that come and go. Someday, however, one of those fads will turn out to be more than a fad—it will become their passion.

4. They Persuade a People.

True leaders eventually attract others to their passion. Sometimes they find others who share the same passion. One thing is sure. Genuine leaders *connect* with others. Leaders, by definition, don't act alone. Their cause is so big, they must empower followers.

Consider Abraham Lincoln. His seemingly impossible cause was twofold: the abolition of slavery and the preservation of the Union. There were times when he had few friends, but he maintained relationships until he attracted enough support to fight for his cause. After much labor, he finally persuaded the right general to take charge of his Union troops. He accomplished both of his causes due to his steady persuasion.

I have already mentioned that my wife and I are working with our kids on their people skills, which begin with courtesy and manners and grow into learning to love people. Ultimately, they must master relationship skills, since it is impossible to separate leaders from relationship.

5. They Pursue a Purpose.

Finally, all genuine leaders find a purpose and pursue it. Job descriptions and time clocks do not motivate or inspire them. They are moved by a sense of mission and vision. Consider President John F. Kennedy. In 1961, he projected that by the end of that decade, NASA would put a man on the moon. He said this at a time when it was technically impossible to do such a thing. But the staff of NASA was captivated by their leader's belief that it was a dream worth chasing. NASA began to double up their efforts. In July of 1969, Neil Armstrong stepped out of Apollo 11 onto the moon, and the dream was fulfilled.

As my kids hit their teenage years, I plan to spend entire days on "dates" together with each one. We will do the "life purpose" exercise found in Chapter Eight. It may be too soon for them to be able to write out a mission statement of their life—but it will be a start to get them thinking and moving in the right direction.

Six Things Your Child Should Do to Get Ready

Last month, I began to evaluate what my children must do to prepare themselves to lead and influence their world. Whether your children are "natural leaders" or "learned leaders," I recommend these six goals for them to pursue.

1. Know Yourself.

This is step one. Children must learn to recognize their own strengths and weaknesses so that they can gravitate toward activities that give them a sense of accomplishment. They must come to love who God has made them to be. It will help them understand where they fit best in organizations and friendships. It will help them identify their style. It will help them to say no to options outside of their strengths. It will also help them develop a healthy self-esteem. Discuss with your child: What makes me unique? What are my strengths and weaknesses as a person? What attracts others to me?

2. Develop Your Gift.

All good leaders conclude what it is they bring to the table that adds value to others. Everyone has something we all need. What does your child have to offer? The sooner a young leader discovers and develops their gift, the sooner they advance in the game of life. Great leaders can identify their ultimate contribution. Some have more than one acquired skill or ability that is unique and valuable. Case in point: As a kid, Jimmy liked to play with his socks and make them talk! Most of the neighborhood children saw him as too strange to befriend. Fortunately, Jimmy's parents allowed him to explore the depths of his creative mind. They thought: *Who knows? Maybe this thing with socks could help him discover his gift!* It did. The boy was Jim Henson, and upon finding his gift, he became a leader in the entertainment field. Just ask his Muppets! Discuss with your kid: What do I do that adds value to others? If I had to narrow it down to one thing, what do others affirm about me more than anything else?

3. Find Your Passion.

Do you remember the movie, *City Slickers*? Billy Crystal is a midlife city slicker who can't figure out life. He talks with "Curly," a crusty old cowboy, who seems to be at peace with himself and the world. When asked how he does it, Curly says the key is to find your "one thing," and the rest will take care of itself. I think Curly is on to something. Your child will solve the motivation problem and usually the money problem when they resolve the issue of passion. Everyone has a passion for something inside of them. Emerging leaders must locate a passion they feel really counts. Discuss with your children: What is it they really want to do? What activities attract them like a magnet?

4. Value People.

In our fast-paced, bottom-line culture, kids must recognize that people are the most important ingredient in the world. Young leaders who value people and learn to connect with them will advance beyond their peers. The ABCs of leadership are simple: **A**ttract people, **B**elieve in people, **C**onnect with people, **D**evelop people, and **E**mpower people. Successful leaders possess these relational skills. If a leader can "get along," others will go along. Discuss with your kids: How important are people to your life? What could you do to communicate to them how valuable they are?

5. Learn Perseverance.

Every young person will fail at something. To be honest, I believe failure is a must. Our obstacles and failures forge our character. Part of leadership development is learning to "keep on keeping on" when things don't go according to plan. When difficulties or obstacles arise, leaders get creative and finish what they start. I wish every young leader could take a course named "Failure 101." We must learn to fail forward, as Dr. John C. Maxwell puts it. Especially in the disposable society in which we live where it is easier to quit the team, walk away from a relationship, resign from the position, or throw away the unused portion of our commitments, kids must learn to press on. Don't rescue them—let them fail. Then, help them up and encourage them to persevere. It is better for them to learn the consequences of failure now than in midlife. Discuss with your kids: Name a time when you refused to quit. How did it make you feel? How did that experience help you?

6. Pursue Excellence.

Excellence is what good leaders introduce to others. Most people don't perform with excellence on their own. They need someone to raise the standard for them. As your children mature, they must understand the importance of doing things with excellence. It takes so little to rise above mediocrity. In baseball, a player who gets up to bat 600 times a season and gets 200 hits will be an all-star. A player who gets up to bat 600 times a season and gets 165 hits is mediocre. That player just needed 35 more hits all season to excel! An Olympic sprinter can finish one-half second behind the winner and receive no medal at all! Excellence is about giving a little extra. The difference that excellence makes, however, is stunning. Think about it. If 99.9 percent were good enough, then . . .

- 2 million documents would be lost by the I.R.S. this year.

- 22,000 checks would be deducted from the wrong bank accounts in the next hour.

- 12 babies would be given to the wrong parents each day.

- 880,000 credit cards would turn out to have wrong information on them.

- 20,000 incorrect drug prescriptions would be written in the next 12 months.

Discuss with your kids: How could you improve the quality of what you do? What would make others notice excellence in your work or play?

PUSH PAUSE

Before you move on to the next chapter, stop and take a deep breath. I recognize I've just given you so much to think about and talk about with your son or daughter. I'm a bit overwhelmed myself as I consider how to best invest in my two children. It's like sitting down to eat an elephant. The good news is—we can do it one bite at a time.

Reflect and Respond

1. On a scale of 1 to 10, how would you rate the natural leadership abilities of your child?

2. What leadership quality or skill most needs to be nurtured in your child?

3. How will you help your kid pursue the goals in this chapter?

7

BECOMING A PERSON OF INFLUENCE

Leadership develops daily, not in a day.
—DR. JOHN C. MAXWELL

JOURNAL ENTRY: OK—so maybe Mom and Dad are right. Maybe I do have some gifts inside me. I can do something great with my life. I just wish I could get on with it. Why do I have to be so patient and wait for everything? I get frustrated at how long it takes to get where I want to go. It's not easy being a kid.

I am like most parents. As my children grow through their stages of maturity, I grow through my own stages as a parent. I move from one parental concern to another as they mature, wondering if I will handle the next one well. Old worries pass. New worries come.

Old Worry: 2 A.M. feedings. New Worry: 2 A.M. dates.

Old Worry: My child will never graduate from high school. New Worry: My child will never go to Harvard.

Old Worry: All too soon he will grow up and leave home. New Worry: He won't.

Seriously, almost all growth happens in stages. Flowers start as bulbs, grow roots, stems, branches, leaves, and buds. Bullfrogs begin as tadpoles. Butterflies start as caterpillars. And leaders start as babies and grow through natural stages as they mature. Years ago, a group of tourists walked through a small Austrian village that was rich in history. When the group noticed a local resident on a corner, they asked him, "Have any famous leaders been born here?" The man smiled. "Nope," he replied, "only babies."

As I have worked with students over the last twenty-two years, I have drawn some simple conclusions about kids and leadership:

1. Leaders are made, not born.

2. Every kid has some leadership potential.

3. Students learn leadership best in community.

4. Leadership development is a process, not an event.

5. In today's world, every student will need to learn leadership.

6. Kids need a coach to help them grow through natural leadership stages.

I want to help you coach your child as they grow through the natural stages of leadership development. You already know they will mature through biological stages. And emotional stages. And intellectual stages, and even spiritual stages. I believe there are also leadership stages they will experience, and the more they understand them, the better they can understand and expedite their own development.

Cameron, a seven-year-old boy, ran out into his backyard one Saturday morning because he heard a parade was coming down Main Street. He loved parades. Fortunately, Main Street was just behind his backyard, and he could hear the music already. Unfortunately, there was a six-foot fence all the way around his yard. Consequently, he watched the parade through a tiny knothole in the fence. It was so small, he could only see whatever was directly in front of him. Then, his father noticed him and decided to help. He hoisted Cameron onto his shoulders and for the first time, the boy could see the panorama of the entire parade.

I want to help you "lift up" your child. They see life through a knothole, spying only what is directly in front of them. I want you to give them a panoramic view of their whole life and enable them to see what kind of steps will help them become an effective leader. This chapter outlines six stages of leadership development that occur over a lifetime. Let's suppose you and I were to sit down over a cup of coffee, and you asked me: What should I expect to happen as my child grows into a leader? I would probably grab a piece of paper and jot down the six stages you're about to read. I'm not sure if anyone walks through them perfectly. They are a goal to shoot for, however, as you hold your kid on your shoulders and give them a vision for leadership. I have given this a bit more structure than normal, so you can identify the stages more clearly. See if you can spot where your child is now.

STAGE ONE: LEADERSHIP FOUNDATIONS

This first stage begins at birth and lasts until your child is old enough to consciously cooperate with their development. In the early childhood phase, most of their growth has much to do with genetics and environment and little to do with their own choices. The first five years of life are crucial because much of their personality and stability takes shape then. Since leadership rests on the stability of the people in charge, it is vital for you, the leadership mentor, to provide a strong leadership foundation during this stage. I call it a leadership foundation because, like a house, the foundation has more to do with the longevity and stability of the structure than anything else.

Have you driven through a subdivision where new homes are being built? If the neighborhood is so new that only concrete slabs are present with a few pipes showing, it doesn't take long to look over the area. Foundations are bland and boring. However, the most boring part of the structure is the most critical to its endurance. This is true also in life. The early years of your child's development are like a concrete slab. The cement is still wet and moldable the first several years. It would be difficult to overestimate the importance of the emotional grounding and sense of security they receive during these years. When my daughter, Bethany, was four years old, she was perched in front of the TV watching Barney. I sat down next to her and began to stroke her hair and tell her how much I loved her. I said again and again, "Bethany—do you know how much I love you? You are my favorite little girl in the world!" She would fidget a little, trying to stay focused on her program. Finally, after voicing my love for about ten minutes, I had irritated her. She replied, "Dad . . . you love me too much." May this always be our children's greatest problem.

What happens when this foundation is not laid well? A boy named Schicklgruber grew up in Europe about one hundred years ago. As a young man, his parents failed to nurture intimacy within him. He was never taught right from wrong. He wasn't hugged or valued. One night, he heard his mom and dad argue about moving away. He was convinced they hated him and suspected they were going to leave him behind. He put an emotional wall up. From then on, he would fend for himself and look out for number one. This boy grew up to be a man. The man grew up to be a leader. You know him as Adolf Hitler.

Landmarks for Stage One.

1. Personality—Temperament, preferences, talents, and style are developing. These will greatly impact their leadership style.

2. Emotional health—Like it or not, the early years determine much of the emotional strength your child will have as an adult leader. Ability determines how far they will go, but stability determines how long they will stay there.

3. Attitude—Leadership is not about position as much as disposition. In these early years, a child becomes predisposed to a mental attitude. It's tough to change it as they get older.

4. Healthy relationships—The social bearings for your child are also set in this early stage. They learn to interact, negotiate, share, and play as a team with others.

Your Part.

In this initial stage of life, the greatest gifts you can give your child are love and consistency. Spend time sharing affection. Skim rocks on a pond, go camping in your basement, or listen to music together. As an emerging leader, they will soak up this love like a sponge and lean on it as they venture into the unsafe world of adolescence. Equally important, however, is to spend time determining the values you will live by. The vital task of parental discipline must be steady. Regardless of how strict you are in your discipline, if your love and boundaries are consistent—your child will fare well. Help them explore the limits of their personality, but recognize security comes from absolute boundaries within the home.

STAGE TWO: LEADERSHIP FORMATION

In the next stage, your child has grown old enough to cooperate with you in their development. This occurs at different ages, but you will know it when you see it. They will begin to care about making decisions and being responsible and about the consequence of their actions. You must establish the priority of character and self-discipline now. Even as they grow in their talents and skills, maintain your focus on their inward growth. Healthy maturity always occurs in this order: "being," "doing," and then "having." Kids want to do it in the reverse order. They want to have, they want to do, then they want to be. Why? Because working on their "being" is so unglamorous. There's no fanfare, no applause, no spotlights. Charisma gets attention. Character usually doesn't. It is true in our adult world, too! Our temptation is to take shortcuts on discipline. We want to bypass these private character issues and jump to the outward skills—the stuff that gets rewarded. When we do this, there is a price to pay.

Once a wealthy man met with a contractor and asked him to build a house. The man gave the builder one-half a million dollars and then gave him a blueprint. He said, "I'm sure you can build this home for less, but I want you to have plenty of money to do the job well. When you are finished building, you can keep whatever money you have left over."

The builder smiled, knowing that he could throw that house together for about thirty thousand dollars. And he did. He put the studs four feet apart, pounded just one nail per board, and slapped on one coat of paint as quickly as he could. He finished in record time. When he returned to the wealthy man, he had a huge wad of money in his pocket. He handed the keys to the man and said, "I'm finished. Here are your keys." The rich man smiled and said, "Oh—I forgot to tell you. The house is yours!"

This is a picture of human nature. The builder thought he was getting ahead but was only cheating himself. We must lead ourselves first. How many leaders have we seen in the last twenty years who have taken short-cuts in their organizations? They rushed ahead, and put production before character. Their gift was bigger than they were. The result? They fell morally, financially, or emotionally. Why? Because stage two was neglected.

Parents who fail to foster character growth in their children send them wrong signals. A Jewish boy grew up during the nineteenth century. His father was nominally committed to his faith and character but only when it was financially profitable for him. When the family moved, their new town wasn't big enough for a synagogue. The father decided he would give up on his faith and join some other group, where he could network with clients. The young boy never forgot his father's hypocrisy and began to see spiritual faith as only a crutch. Money ruled the world. The young boy was Karl Marx. His communist theories have robbed individuals of freedom for almost one hundred years.

Landmarks for Stage Two.

1. Self-discipline—In this stage, children must learn to do what is right, even when they don't feel like it. They must choose to do what they should do, not what they want to do.

2. Identity—Good leadership always comes from a solid sense of our identity. An emerging leader must have a healthy self-image and be OK with who they are and are not.

3. Values—This stage is when kids should embrace values and core beliefs. These become the moral compass by which they will make decisions. Leadership is always based on values.

4. Responsibility—Your child must learn to be responsible for their actions. They must discern what is right and own up to the conse-quences of bad decisions.

Your Part.

The greatest gift you can give your child in this stage is to reward good character. They will be tempted to take shortcuts and do things that gain the applause of people. Remember: what gets rewarded gets done. Reward their private disciplines, their good decisions, their sense of responsibility, and their commitments. Consider the house analogy again for a moment. Our kids have to learn to build the infrastructure of the house before they can put on the paint and decorate it. This stage involves the internal framework: the studs, the nails, the pipes, and the load-bearing beams that will hold the house up when storms rage. We can't see those studs or nails—but we know they are there when a storm blows through. It isn't the nice-looking trim or paint that holds the house together, even though they are visible. Don't let your kid be fooled. Like the paint, their talents are visible and important. But without character, they will fall over with the house in bad weather.

STAGE THREE: LEADERSHIP FITNESS

Through adolescence and their young adult years, something happens in kids. A marked difference occurs in how they learn best. They've sat and listened in their classrooms for years. As they enter this stage, the primary way they learn is through *experience.* They must begin to practice what they know. That's why I call this phase "leadership fitness." In order to continue growing as a leader, they must exercise what they have learned. If they don't, they will stunt their growth. Teens get antsy. They intuitively know they should get up and discover their gifts. They want to explore the unknown. More than 50 percent of teens participate in community service projects on a regular basis. In an interview, one student said he felt it was his obligation to serve and give back to society! (There's a novel attitude.)

Andrew Leary was a high-school student who was given a life-changing school project. He was to research the problem of hunger in America. He discovered that hunger was not only an issue nationwide, but also in his own New Jersey town. To assess the scope of the problem, Andrew and his classmates organized a one-day "Harvest Festival" where they gave away more than sixty meals and one thousand pounds of food, along with survey questionnaires. Over the next six months, his team collected additional data and presented its case to 130 community members. As a result, adults and students joined together to build a soup kitchen. Andrew represented a task force before the news media, community groups, and the county planning board. He also helped to raise $35,000 to operate the facility. Harvest House is now up and running on a permanent basis, serving lunch five days a week. "This project taught me that even though I am a high school student, I have the vision and ability to change lives," said Andrew later, as quoted on the Prudential Community Awards Web site. "I learned that standing up for what you believe in is not always easy, but through perseverance you can accomplish your goals."

Another teenager, Brett Byrd, also made his mark. He and his brother raised more than $100,000 in his mother's memory for the prevention of breast cancer. The death of his mother caused Brett to get serious about his musical gift and use it for a purpose. Working in conjunction with the American Cancer Society, the boys have played in dozens of concerts and spoken to thousands of people about cancer and about how to get by when a parent dies. This has not only helped the boys get through a difficult time, but also helped others in need. They hope to eventually raise one million dollars for the fight against breast cancer. (You can read more about their story on the Prudential Community Awards Web site.)[1]

Landmarks for Stage Three.

1. Discovery of gifts—As they explore and experiment with activities, kids should begin to explore their primary talents and gifts. They should know their strengths and weaknesses.

2. People skills—Leadership cannot be divorced from relationships. At this stage, emerging leaders should learn how to relate, communicate, and motivate others to cooperate.

3. Vision—This is the optimal stage for kids to begin catching a vision. As they see needs, they should begin to investigate ideas and see how those needs could be addressed.

4. Sacrifice—In this stage, one crucial lesson involves surrendering options in their life that hinder them from reaching their potential. They must sacrifice in order to become a "contributor," not just a "consumer," in groups.

The Leadership Triangle

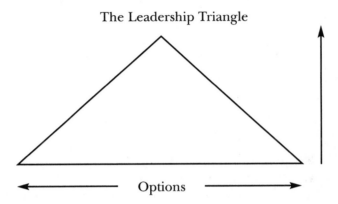

Options

Growing up into leadership works much like this triangle. The base represents our range of options. In our younger years, we had lots of options, lots of freedom in our lives. We could do whatever we wanted as a young child. As we mature into leadership, we willingly give up those "rights" or options in order to serve people and reach our goals. Exercising these rights isn't bad; it just prevents us from giving our all to a cause. The higher we grow into leadership, the more we must sacrifice. We must give up to go up.

Your Part.

This stage marks a major crossroad for young leaders. Many get side-tracked at this stage. They are either unwilling to "exercise" their leadership muscles, or they refuse to make the sacrifices necessary to grow up as a leader. They'll do what they know to do, or they won't—and they'll stop growing as a leader. Your action is required at this stage. The best way you can help your child is to walk with them into the arena of action, if necessary. Talk about their choices. Help them start practicing with their leadership gifts. Aid in their exploration of and experimentation with a community cause, such as washing cars to raise money for heart disease or walking a marathon to raise funds for diabetes research. Help them communicate better in relationships. Teach them it is normal to fail. They are young adults, and it is healthy for them to take responsibility, take risks, and take action.

STAGE FOUR: LEADERSHIP FRUITFULNESS

At this stage, your child is no longer living under your roof. At least, not in most circumstances. An emerging leader hits this stage from the young adult years through midlife, and success is based on how well the first three stages have been mastered. They have wrestled with the issues of identity, discipline, and abilities. Now, they experience the payoff. Like Tiger Woods and his passion for golf, the earlier they start, the earlier they become proficient at leadership. Now they see the fruit of labor and leadership.

Think back to our house analogy. This stage represents the work on the exterior of the house. The internal framework is already set—now everyone can see what the house has become. When the house is built well, it is not only beautiful to look at but provides secure covering from the weather. Both function and form are present.

I will be the first to admit this is an optimal scenario. Bookstores have carried dozens of books on the subject of "midlife crisis" ever since baby boomers have been turning forty. Their crises, however, could have been avoided for the most part. For instance, when a businessman hits midlife and feels he must divorce his wife, find a new, pretty young thing, buy a cherry-red Ferrari, and drop his career in order to be fulfilled—something is wrong with his development. I believe he has failed to sufficiently grow through the first three stages of his life. Now, at forty, he experiences midlife crises instead of midlife fruitfulness. This is an unnecessary tragedy.

Landmarks for Stage Four.
1. Priorities—By this stage, leaders must determine what their top priorities are and stick to them. They know what behaviors produce external results and internal reward.

2. Empowerment and delegation—Effective leaders don't fulfill their mission by themselves. They learn to equip others to share the load; to empower them by delegating suitable tasks.

3. Motives—In this stage, a leader should have matured past wrong motives. They are no longer people-pleasers. They don't pursue fame or success but fulfillment and significance.

4. Strategic thinking—As they grow, leaders mature past doing good things to doing the best things in their field. Strategy determines their moves. They are proactive, not reactive.

Their Part.

While you're still their parent, I want to discuss their role more than yours here. Their part in this stage of the journey will require them to gain as much wisdom as they can. This is a stage where they "narrow their wedge" and determine the "one thing" they do best in their leadership. Lasting leaders are not a jack-of-all-trades but a master of one. Even when they can do more than one, they narrow it down to a few. At this stage, leaders are wise enough to know that while they can do anything, they can't do everything. They zero in on the one to three activities that really make a difference. This furnishes them with perspective when things get tough, the stock market drops, or technology introduces a whole new way of doing what they do.

STAGE FIVE: LEADERSHIP FOCUS

Many seek but few find the "leadership focus" stage of the leadership journey. Based on personal strengths and weaknesses, opportunities, and network, leaders make moves that position them to do what they were built to do. They begin to understand their ultimate contribution in life. It may mean a job change or a geographical move. It may mean taking a risky step based on a gut feeling more than a good pension plan. It could mean making an internal move, rather than a change of locations, where an attitude adjustment changes everything. In any case, it is usually a step taken from the heart, after much soul-searching and prayer. When a leader makes the move, however, it enables him to flourish.

One of my primary mentors is Dr. John C. Maxwell. I believe he is in stage five of his leadership journey. He was a good pastor for twenty-six years. In 1995, however, he resigned from the church he pastored to lead our organization, the INJOY Group, full-time in Atlanta. It was a marvelous move for him as a leader. He now equips leaders all over the world and has since written a number of best-selling books on leadership. This is his niche. He was a good pastor—but he is a great leadership trainer. I believe he is now making his ultimate contribution.

In this stage, the leader, the work, and the context all converge for a maximum fit. In other words, who the leader is, what the leader does, and who they do it with come together for a perfect match. Inside, all leaders long for this, but most haven't prepared themselves for it. They have failed to grow through the stages well. The good news is—this stage awaits all who prepare for it.

If we return to our house analogy, stage five represents those ingredients of a home that are personal finishing touches, those that make the house novel and unique. They give it personality and flair. It might be adding a deck, or some trim around the siding, or even a patio or porch. Now—the house is complete. It is a grand statement of the person who lives in it. It enables the homeowner to enjoy all the years of labor they have invested in it.

Landmarks for Stage Five.

1. Maximum effectiveness—In this season, a leader does not merely have a job; they "do a work." What they do and how they do it provide measurable effectiveness.

2. Wisdom and perspective—Leaders work smarter, not just harder. A byproduct of this stage is knowing what kind of legacy you will leave and how to best pursue it.

3. Leadership development—A leader can only reproduce who they are. In this stage, the leader is committed to personal growth and multiplying other leaders.

4. Mission—By this stage, leaders live on mission. They have a sense of destiny and embrace it. They see the big picture and how their work fits into it.

Their Part.

This is likely a stage that neither you nor your child has experienced yet. The leader's role is to lead from their mission. They must see the big picture, develop other leaders, surround themselves with like visionaries, work smart, and enjoy the ride. At this point, the leadership journey is most satisfying. I say this to whet the appetite of your son or daughter to continue forging ahead, knowing that great days await them.

STAGE SIX: LEADERSHIP FINALE

The final stage of this optimal leadership journey is what I call the leadership finale, which generally occurs in the twilight years of a leader's life. Silver hair becomes a crown for their head, and they enjoy living life from the overflow of their influence. In fact, in this stage, leaders don't have to look for opportunities to impact others. Others seek them out for mentoring relationships and advice. I know of several "seasoned" leaders that I consider to be in this stage. Fred Smith, the founder of Federal Express, is in this stage. He is an older gentleman who has lived and led with integrity, innovation, and productivity. He has the respect of many. When he speaks in front of other leaders, everyone is taking notes! Dr. Billy Graham is another such leader. This spiritual leader has held to his personal vision of sharing the love of God with every nation in the world. He has demonstrated character and vision. Now, younger leaders just want to get close to him. Regardless of how simple his message is, it is profound simply because it comes from his lips.

If you reach this stage, it doesn't mean you'll be famous or write a best-selling book. It simply means that those who do know you respect you greatly. They follow you. You've become a person of influence. This is my aspiration for myself and my kids.

Landmarks for Stage Six.

1. Deep influence—In this final stage, leaders possess a deep and wide span of influence, often greater than they realize. They may impact people they don't even know.

2. Poise—Seasoned leaders are unmoved by flattery or insults. They are poised and living out the life they were meant to live. They are steadied by their sense of mission.

3. Fulfillment—At this point, the reward of the leader is the journey itself. The leader can see their influence and cherish how many they get to invest in as emerging leaders.

4. Mentoring—One of the best uses of their time is mentoring apprentices who seek them out. They spend the majority of their time multiplying their leadership wisdom in others.

WHERE ARE YOU? WHERE IS YOUR CHILD?

Do you recognize what we just did in this chapter? We walked through the entire life of a leader. I trust you can see where you are in the (optimal) journey and where your child is now. These stages are not meant to overwhelm your child but to whet their appetite for what could happen if they continue "building" the leader already inside of them.

Reflect and Respond

1. Which stage do you believe your child is in?

2. What landmark issues are they facing?

3. How could you help your children settle the issues they are facing now?

8

CROSSING THE SEVEN CS
TO LEADERSHIP

There are no illegitimate children—only illegitimate parents.
—JUDGE LEON YANKWICH, 1928

JOURNAL ENTRY: Every day I write in this journal. I think I'm in a rut. I don't seem to be growing at all. At least, I can't tell if I'm growing. My grandparents say they're proud of me. They say they can see a big difference in me every time they are with me. They think I am mature for my age. I just wish I could see it.

I heard a cute story.

A preacher and a taxi cab driver from New York both died and went to heaven on the same day. There stood St. Peter, just like they'd always imagined, at the Pearly Gate. Peter suggested, "Well, fellas, since you both died the same day, why don't I usher you to your mansions together?"

Both men agreed. Peter told the cab driver he would start with him. They all walked upward to cloud number eighty-seven, and there stood a luxurious mansion. It was huge. Ornate. Sparkling. St. Peter said, "Well, here you go." The cab driver was elated and strutted in through the front door. About that time, the preacher began to ponder what just happened.

He thought: *Wow! If that New York cabbie just got a beautiful mansion like that—I wonder what I'm going to get? I served the Lord faithfully for over fifty years!*

St. Peter turned to the preacher and motioned for him to follow him to his mansion. They walked downward to cloud number four. There in front of them stood a tiny, old, one-room shack! It looked miserable. When Peter informed the preacher it belonged to him, the clergyman was livid with anger. "You gave a luxurious mansion to a cab driver from New York, but you are giving me a tiny, one-room shack? I want an explanation for this!"

Peter just smiled. "Well, it's like this. Heaven is interested in results." He paused, as the preacher nodded in agreement. Peter continued: "When you preached, people just slept. But when that man drove—people prayed!"

I chuckle whenever I think of that story. There is a kernel of truth to it. Heaven is, indeed, interested in results. And so is your employer. So is every sports fan, when it comes to their favorite team. So are salespeople who sell products day after day. What counts is not their activity but their productivity. We are no different as moms and dads. At some point, we have to evaluate the fruit of our labor as parents, too.

At the same time, we have to admit that sometimes growth is hard to measure. Leadership success isn't merely about selling lots of widgets or collecting more followers. A salesman of widgets isn't always a leader, and Hitler had loads of followers—but he wasn't the kind of leader we want to reproduce. Consequently, in order to measure leadership growth, we have to go deeper than evaluating externals.

CROSSING THE SEVEN CS

Let's push the pause button and evaluate your child's leadership growth. You've waded through loads of material in the first seven chapters of this book. Let's stop now and measure the central qualities that healthy, effective, lasting leaders possess. I'll begin with a list of seven characteristics that all begin with the letter *C.* If your sons and daughters score well in these qualities—they are well on their way to becoming leaders. This list of characteristics is timeless and universal and measures both your leadership and that of your children. Let's dig in.

1. Character.

Character is the sum total of a leader's personal identity, emotional security, ethics and values, and self-discipline. Strong character enables leaders to possess integrity, to earn trust, to gain respect, to experience consistency, and to communicate credibility. High-school student Shelarese Ruffin worked at a drug prevention agency in Atlanta. As she read about the thousands of drug addicts who dropped out of high school, she felt she had to do something. Shelarese researched the issue and came up with some creative solutions, notably one to help at-risk teens. She successfully applied for a $50,000 grant, and after just two years, her program has helped more than three thousand students and expanded to other states. It all started with a seventeen-year-old student. As you think about your own character, consider these questions:

- I assume responsibility for myself and my team.
- I am secure in my identity and my self-esteem.
- I do what I should even when I don't feel like it.
- I have convictions that I stand for in public.

Character is the foundation we build our leadership upon. When we have this foundation in place, we can move on to building other necessary qualities.

2. Compassion.

While the issue of character deals with the world's perception of a leader, compassion deals with the leader's perception of others in the world. Compassion moves a leader to demonstrate generosity and to meet the needs of others. Sagen Woolery, age twelve, saw a TV commercial about free school lunch programs for needy families. Sagen wondered where children who depend on the free lunch program at school eat lunch during the summer. Her mother introduced her to the director of a local soup kitchen, who helped her act on her compassion. Sagen planned menus and solicited donations for food and money to start her own summer meal service for needy kids and their families. "Kid's Kitchen" has served 3,200 people in her community. Sagen is quoted on the Prudential Community Awards Web site as saying, "I think we are all responsible for each other." How well do you express compassion for others? Does compassion move you to meet the needs of others and help solve problems? Respond to the following:

- I am sensitive to spot the needs of others.

- I will help those in need even when it costs me.

- I am moved emotionally by my love for others.

- I'm fulfilled when I serve and meet others' needs.

Once compassion moves you to serve others, you'll be required to demonstrate courage enough to take a risk and act. Take a look at the next quality, courage.

3. Courage.

Once character has been developed to include compassion for others, it takes courage to implement change. All leaders demonstrate courage. Courage enables the leader to step out and take risks; it initiates action. Courage allows leaders to endure unfamiliar territory and embrace the unknown. When leaders display "vision in action," it is contagious. Just ask Subaru Takahashi of Japan. The fourteen-year-old set sail on a daring journey from Tokyo to San Francisco in a thirty-foot boat. With his parents' blessing, he planned and trained to cross the Pacific Ocean—alone. Along the trip, an engine died, killing power to his electric generator, and his radio battery failed. He braved the rest of the trip with no lights and no contact with others. He persevered and became the youngest person to sail solo across the Pacific Ocean. As a leader, he's captured the spirit of other daring young adventurers, who want to join him on future trips![1] How well do you exhibit courage? Take a moment and evaluate yourself:

- I like to start new projects, even when it's scary.

- People think I'm a brave person.

- I don't mind being the first to take a risk.

- When ideas arise, I want to take action, not talk.

At this point, a leader must measure not only their ability to step out and take action, but what kind of ability they possess to meet the needs of others. Eventually, people will evaluate the competency of their leader.

4. Competency.

A leader of character must be capable of convincing followers that he or she is competent enough to get the job done. Competency builds on the foundations of compassion and courage; the will is in the spirit, now the flesh must not be weak! A competent leader has the ingenuity and creativity to figure out what to do and how to do it in order to get results.

Jarrett Mynear, who was diagnosed with cancer five times in nine years, is such an example. The details of his leadership story, briefly summed up here, appear on the Prudential Spirit of Community Awards Web site.[2] While undergoing a bone marrow transplant, he received a toy from a group of adult volunteers. "I remember how good it felt to realize someone who didn't even know me was thinking of me during my hospital stay," he said. After careful planning, he wrote a business plan, approached the hospital board for approval, solicited donors, developed toy lists, obtained community endorsements, opened a bank account, and invited the media to a ribbon-cutting ceremony for "Jarrett's Joy Cart," which provides toys for children at a cancer center in Kentucky—at age eleven! His leadership competency and conviction are an inspiration to us all. Jarrett's business plan was implemented successfully because of a young leader's competency.

Have you stopped to evaluate your level of competency? What abilities do you bring to the table?

- My ideas often turn into plans
- I have some unique and useful abilities
- I can figure out how to finish a job I start
- I am good at solving problems

Once you determine your primary competencies, you'll have to demonstrate convictions in order to stick with them until you see results. Take a moment and reflect on your convictions.

5. Convictions.

A conviction is a strong belief in a principle that enables a leader to take a stand and guide them into the future. Convictions usually revolve around the values a leader embraces. Perhaps they believe in human rights, and this conviction moves them to raise awareness of the slave trade going on in Sudan, Africa. Convictions are stronger than opinions or ideas. A leader knows what he believes in, makes sacrifices because of his convictions, shows others how strongly he feels about these beliefs, and acts on them. Leaders embrace their convictions and live—and sometimes die—for them. I'm sure you remember Cassie Burnall, a student at Columbine High School. She stood for her conviction despite the consequences. She died because she valued her convictions more than her life. Martin Luther King Jr. once said: "If a man hasn't discovered something that he will die for, he isn't fit to live." May I ask you a personal question? As a leader, what are you willing to die for? Are you a person of convictions? Consider how much these statements apply to you.

- I know exactly what I believe in
- I make sacrifices because of my beliefs
- Others can see I feel strongly about some things
- Passion enables me to act on what I believe

Commitment works hand in hand with conviction. I don't think we can effectively lead anyone without a measure of commitment to what we believe. Let's measure the quality of our commitment as a leader.

6. Commitment.

All effective leaders possess strong commitment. They understand few things get done without perseverance and have the ability to engage a project until it is completed. Commitment is needed most when a leader encounters routine obstacles or unsettling failures. I don't know a leader who hasn't faced at least one failure or obstacle. Just ask Joshua Marcus. Joshua visited a local child-care center for disadvantaged children and was moved by the many needs he saw there. He asked staff members what the children needed most. They said the kids needed backpacks and basic school supplies.

Joshua came up with the idea for "Sack It to You," a nonprofit group that provides backpacks filled with school supplies for kids. His idea didn't exactly catch on at first. He wrote letters to backpack manufacturers but got little response. In fact, his first few attempts to gain support from suppliers failed. But Josh didn't give up. He finally got a big donation from Office Depot—enough to outfit every kid at the child-care center. He has now raised $20,000, part of it from his own bar mitzvah money. Now that's true commitment and leadership! How do you measure up? Are you committed to anything as a young leader? Consider these statements.

- I am stubborn and don't give up easily

- I finish what I start

- Obstacles don't discourage me but challenge me

- I can stay focused on one goal

There's one more *C* I think we should consider. It deals with how we connect with other people in order to take them on the journey with us.

7. Charisma.

The final leadership characteristic, charisma, enables leaders to accomplish more. This topic, mystical to many, is often misunderstood. Charisma enables leaders to connect with others. It enhances a leader's communication skills and magnetically draws followers to a cause. Marcus Houston is a vivid example of this truth. Marcus, a high-school student in Denver, developed an educational program called "Just Say Know." It teaches middle-school students what it takes to succeed in high school. Marcus reflected on what enabled him to succeed, took his message to younger students, and connected with the students in a marvelous way. To date, he has connected with more than eight hundred students and plans to expand nationally. Competent leaders can accomplish more if they empower others through their charisma. Leaders do no one any good if they're competent, but can't connect with others. What do you possess that attracts others to you or helps you connect with them? Think about your response to these statements. Do they describe you?

- I attract people—they like to be around me
- When I enter a room, I think of others, not myself
- I give confidence and encouragement to others
- I am genuinely interested in other people

You have now crossed the seven Cs of leadership. It's important to view these qualities as acquired characteristics that need to be developed, rather than assuming they are personality traits that cannot be acquired. All seven are crucial to learning leadership and even more crucial to mentoring others to be leaders.

Before we finish this chapter, let's explore two other checklists that will help you discover your leadership style and strengths.

YOUR ATTRACTION ASSETS

You may already know your IQ (your intelligence quotient). More important to your leadership capabilities, however, is your influence quotient. This is

ATTRACTION ASSET	VOLUME

1. Passion and Enthusiasm
   You possess an energy and excitement
   that encourages and ignites others. 1 2 3 4 5 6 7 8 9 10

2. Insight and Wisdom
   You are discerning and understand
   situations and people, which causes
   others to listen to you. 1 2 3 4 5 6 7 8 9 10

3. Relational Charisma
   You have a warm and magnetic
   personality that others love to be
   around and makes them feel safe. 1 2 3 4 5 6 7 8 9 10

4. Productive Ability
   People naturally follow you because
   you accomplish your goals efficiently;
   you get the job done. 1 2 3 4 5 6 7 8 9 10

5. Character and Courage
   You do what is right even when
   it is difficult. This causes
   people to trust you. 1 2 3 4 5 6 7 8 9 10

6. Communication Skills
   You express your thoughts and ideas
   clearly and effectively, motivating
   others to go along with you. 1 2 3 4 5 6 7 8 9 10

7. Gifts and Talents
   You have natural abilities that others
   admire. Those gifts draw them to
   support you. 1 2 3 4 5 6 7 8 9 10

based on your "attraction assets." Everyone has something inside them that attracts others to them: It may be your charisma. It may be your honesty. It may be your skills. Have you ever asked yourself: Why would others follow me? Mentors and leaders-to-be can use this checklist to reconsider: what you assumed your strengths were before reading this book, where your developing strengths are now, and where you see your leadership qualities developing in the next year after investing time with mentoring.

Good leaders give others as many reasons to follow them as they can. The more attraction assets you possess, the more variety and volume of people seem to follow you.

THE LIFE THEY WERE MEANT TO LIVE

My final checklist may be the most important one. You and your child should reflect and answer these questions after careful thought. Their answers to them will help them uncover their God-given purpose in life and determine the direction of their future leadership. Remember: when they find their purpose and gifts—their leadership will naturally flow.

The older your child is, the easier it will be to respond to this checklist. Depending on your child's age, this list may be premature right now. If so, lay it aside for a later date. Take it slowly and sit down several times if necessary in order to cover it all. They may need a few sheets of paper to contain their thoughts and ideas. Afterward, summarize common threads in answers. With your mentoring, this exercise will help them understand and create a purpose statement for their life. You both may be surprised at what you discover!

1. Passion and Burdens.

What ideas do I feel compelled to go after? When I watch the news, do certain stories make me emotional or cause me to become passionate— and make me want to do something?

2. Talents and Abilities.

What natural talents do I possess? Do I have any God-given abilities like art, organization, music, working with my hands, speaking, or other skills that I could use in the future?

3. Life-changing Factors.

What events and people have shaped my life so far? What would make my list if I wrote down top mentors, books, awards, negative and positive experiences that have impacted me?

4. Results.

What produces the most when I do it? Of all the activities I participate in, which ones am I really good at that seem to bear fruit? What do I do that gets results?

5. Inward Desires.

What would I do if I had no fear of failure? When I think about what is in my heart, what do I really want to do with my life?

6. Major Themes.

What subjects seem to keep coming up in my conversations? Are there recurring themes that I have a lot to say about, when they arise?

7. Fulfillment and Satisfaction.

What do I deeply enjoy doing? Are there activities that give me the feeling: this is what I was built to do? What makes me feel most fulfilled?

8. Dreams and Vision.

What do I dream about doing? What aspirations continue to be clear in my mind? When I think about the future, do I seem to be drawn toward a certain vision?

9. Recognition and Affirmation.

What do others say about me? When I talk to those who know me well, what do they recognize as gifts and strengths in my life? What do they seem to notice and compliment?

10. *Circumstances and Opportunity.*

What is in front of me right now as an opportunity? Instead of making life complex, what if I simply ask: Do I have opportunities right under my nose that I haven't seen before?

A LIFE SENTENCE

I recommend that you spend a day together responding to this with your son or daughter. Travel somewhere you can be alone such as a quiet local park, go over these lists, with a pad of paper and a pencil. Respond to the questions as honestly as possible. The answers will enable your child to make heartfelt choices based on a purpose that fits their identity, rather than based on paychecks or family expectations.

Next, help your child write out a "life sentence" or at least begin with one to three purpose statements based on their gifts and passion. It should be memorable and measurable, and it should reflect life's big picture as much as possible. I recognize it will change as they grow older and understand more about themselves—but it will help them get started in the right direction. It will help them choose courses, mentors, books, and activities based on their strengths.

I know one young man who recently wrote out his life sentence after a weekend retreat with his church youth group. As a committed Christian, he believes his purpose is:

> "To use my talents in art and athletics to help others begin a personal relationship with God and to tear down walls between racial groups."

Have your child hang their life sentence on their bedroom wall where they can see it every day. Talk about it. Pray about it. Review it at least once a year to make any necessary adjustments. This will set them up to succeed and lead from their strengths. In fact, all three of these evaluations are designed to provide helpful feedback to your child on who they really are and what they should do in order to lead others effectively.

DREAM BIG, DREAM RIGHT

One of the greatest gifts you can give your child is the permission to dream big and dream "right." We must help them pursue a vision larger than themselves, but also one that fits who they are. Dr. John C. Maxwell wrote: "Leaders must leave their comfort zone, but not their gift zone."

When we do this, we take the lid off of our children. We give them permission to spread their wings and fly—perhaps higher than we have as parents. This prevents them from falling into the pit of mediocrity. Average children don't exist. If my kids become average adults, it is because I have not helped them flourish in their purpose. Listen to these words from a twelve-year-old boy, who struggled through such an experience and put his thoughts on paper.

THE AVERAGE CHILD

I don't cause teachers trouble, my grades have been OK,
I listen in my classes, and I'm in school every day.
My teachers think I'm average, my parents think so, too.
I wish I didn't know that, 'cause there's lots I'd like to do.
I'd like to build a rocket—I have a book that tells you how,
Or start a stamp collection. Well, no use in trying now.
'Cause since I found I'm average, I'm just smart enough you see,
To know there's nothing special I should expect of me.
I'm part of that majority, that bump part of the bell . . .
Who spends his life unnoticed in an average kind of hell.

Anonymous

Reflect and Respond

1. In which of the seven Cs is your child strong? Where is your child weak?

2. What are your child's primary "attraction assets"?

3. Can you tell what your child's primary gift and purpose in life might be?

PART 3

WHEN TO SEIZE THE MOMENT

9

WHAT MOSES TAUGHT US ABOUT TEACHING OUR KIDS

Children have a much better chance of growing up if their parents have done so first.
—SUSAN PETERS

LAST NIGHT MY WIFE, PAM, AND I BOTH HAD chores to do. It was growing late, and the house was a mess. Our kids were tired from a long week but were not even remotely interested in going to bed. It was evident they needed sleep from their attitudes. Pam was counting on me to tuck them in, but I was preoccupied with a project that refused to be completed. I was determined to get it done. Both of us were at the end of our ropes when we had to tell our kids three times to brush their teeth and get in bed! Seeing that this scene could escalate into a yelling match, I escorted the kids up the stairs. I just wanted them in bed as quickly as possible. This night, there would not be much talk time. Not much prayer time. I was short and to the point.

Later, as I was crawling into bed myself, I reflected on the evening. This was not the kind of atmosphere I want to experience in my home. I hate it when I am reactionary as a parent. I hate playing defense with my time, rather than offense. I don't want to be satisfied with mere survival; I can't be happy just to make it through the day and fail to truly mentor my children.

I recognize that every family has tough days—but my schedule is so full this year, I knew this would be the norm for us, unless I got a handle on it.

I heard about a young mother who had just given birth to her fourth child. After friends gave her a baby shower, she sent a thank-you note to them. Her words surprised them: "Many thanks for the play pen. It is being used every day, from 2:00 to 3:00 P.M. I get in to read, and the children can't get near me!"

After our hectic evening, Pam and I talked about being proactive again, in our parenting. Like you, we want to create good memories and invest in our kids so that they have the tools to be proactive leaders in their world. In order to do this, we need a plan.

WHAT MOSES HAS TO SAY

Fortunately, help often comes from the most surprising places. Almost four thousand years ago, the Jewish people were returning to their homeland in Israel. They had been slaves for centuries in Egypt. Now, they would experience a freedom that they had only heard about from their parents and grandparents. Many of the younger ones needed to be reconnected to their heritage. They needed a leader to help them get established as a people.

Moses was their leader. In the Pentateuch (the first five books of the Scriptures), he wrote about parenting. He specifically taught the Jewish parents how they were to instruct their kids. Although his words are four millennia old, they are as relevant today as they were back then. In the sixth chapter of the book of Deuteronomy, Moses wrote about how to pass on values to children. His advice is simple but profound.

Reggie Joiner, founder of FamilyWise, summarized the five major principles Moses taught in this passage of Scripture. They are gripping for me, as a dad who wants to become more proactive in my parenting. See if they don't grip you, as well.

1. It Doesn't Matter What You Know, If You Don't Know What Matters.

Listen to Moses, in Deuteronomy 6:4: "Hear, O Israel: The LORD our God, the LORD is one!"

It's such a simple phrase. It hardly seems worth repeating. All good Jews know it and have based their entire law upon it. That's the very reason why the principle is so powerful. The timeless truth for us today is not hard to spot. It doesn't matter what you know if you don't know what matters.

Good parenting and good leadership development always begin with some central truths. These principles are the foundation. They matter the most. Everything we learn about the daily grind is good, but meaningless if we don't communicate the big picture stuff that really counts. We can only be proactive when we have settled the issues we believe are important. If we fail to do this, we can only react and do damage control. If we forget the ultimate, we become slaves to the immediate.

According to *Group Magazine,* when researchers asked mothers to keep a record of how many times their children whined for something, they found the average was five times a day—every single day. Even worse, these mothers reported almost half of their purchases directly resulted from their kids pestering them. No wonder some teenagers have a hard time saying no to cigarettes, illegal drugs, alcohol, and sex.[1] They see their parents giving in so easily.

Have you settled what really matters in life? Do you know what is most important, and have you communicated it to your kids? It's a little bit like having a compass on board a ship, when you are in the middle of the Atlantic Ocean. As you grope through the dark nights out at sea, it won't matter that you know what color your boat is or how many bolts were used to put it together. What matters is what direction you are headed. The compass is the key.

I believe there are four main areas that really matter as I help my kids navigate life:

1. Priorities—What is important?

2. Problems—How do you react to them?

3. People—How do you treat them?

4. Philosophy—How do you view life?

When it comes to knowing what matters for leadership development, I suggest the four primary colors of a leader (mentioned in Chapter Five):

character, perspective, courage, and favor. From these four qualities, all the other leadership skills radiate.

When Moses brought up what mattered most, he listed two items: "the LORD [is] our God" and "He is one." The stuff that matters most should *not* be a long list of countless things. What matters most should be a handful of principles that are central to life and goals.

2. The Relationship Is More Important Than the Rules.

The next thing Moses says is: "You shall love the LORD your God with all your heart, with all your soul, and with all your strength."

This is difficult for some parents to understand. Regardless of how important you feel the rules are, relationship is always more important. God didn't say "keep My rules with all your heart" although He gave them Ten Commandments. His first priority as a heavenly Father was love between His child and Him. Regardless of how poorly or how well our kids do with the house rules—we must always put our relationship with them first.

Rules are not bad. They just don't transform a heart. They change behavior from the outside in, rather than the inside out. Love changes the heart and motives of a person. Love can get a person to do what a law can never get them to do. Consequently, we need to know the first and right place for rules. This is my " first" rule for rules. They should be:

F—FEW. The more you have, the tougher it is to keep and enforce them.

I—IMPORTANT. You should only create them if they are important to family life.

R—RELEVANT. Make sure they serve a relevant need and aren't outdated.

S—SIMPLE. Your child should be able to remember and share them in one sentence.

T—TRANSFORMING. The rules should work to help shape the values of your child.

I have found the better my relationship is with my kids, the easier it is for them to keep the rules, and the less they need them. As a child matures, their need for rules should diminish. They never grow out of the need for relationship. This is what enables them to accomplish great things—someone who believes in them, encourages them, and resources them. I love the story of the first-grade boy who strutted up in front of his classmates and proclaimed, "When I grow up, I'm going to be a lion tamer. I'll have lots of fierce lions, and I'll walk in the cage, and they'll roar!" He paused a minute, looking at his classmates' faces, then added: "Of course, I'll have my mother with me."

A college professor had his sociology class go into the Baltimore slums to gather case histories of two hundred young boys. They were asked to write their evaluation of each boy's future prospects. In every case, the students wrote: "He hasn't got a chance."

Twenty-five years later, another sociology professor came across the earlier study. He had his students follow up on the project to see what had happened. With the exception of twenty boys who had moved away or died, the students learned that 176 of the remaining 180 had achieved extraordinary success as lawyers, doctors, and businessmen.

The professor was astounded and decided to pursue the matter further. Fortunately, all the men lived in the area, and he was able to ask each one: "How do you account for your success?" In each case, those men replied with feeling: "There was a teacher . . . "

The teacher was still alive, so the professor sought her out and asked the elderly but still alert lady what magic formula she had used to pull these boys out of the slums into success. The teacher's eyes sparkled, and her lips broke into a gentle smile. "It's really very simple," she said. "I loved those boys."

Kids learn best from those with whom they have a positive relationship. You can impress your kids from a distance, but influence is born out of relationship. Leaders must learn the priority of relationships, and I believe this is best learned at home.

3. It Has to Be in You Before It Can Be in Them.

Then, Moses said: "And these words which I command you today shall be in your heart" (Deut. 6:6).

Moses was speaking to the parents. Before he told them how to teach principles to their kids, he said the principles have to reside inside the hearts of the parents. In other words, you can't give away what you don't have! Walk the talk. It has to be in you before it can be in them. And, if it doesn't work at home, don't try to export it.

Perhaps the best exercise for you, as a parent, is to ask yourself: What leadership qualities and skills do I naturally model? These you will pass on whether you try to or not. Your kids will catch your lifestyle. Next, ask: Which leadership qualities and skills do I lack but need to possess, because they are so critical for my child to learn? We teach what we know, but we reproduce what we are.

You may remember the story of the frail old man who went to live with his son, daughter-in-law, and four-year-old grandson. The old man's hands trembled, his eyesight blurred, and his step faltered. When the family ate together, the old man's shaky hands and failing eyesight made it difficult for him. Peas rolled off his spoon onto the floor. When he picked up his glass, milk spilled on the tablecloth. And he kept breaking the dishes! His son became irritated with the mess and decided to set up a small table in the corner for Grandpa. To prevent the old man from breaking dishes, his son gave him a wooden bowl to eat from.

When they ate together now, it was calm. The son would glance over to see his old man and notice a tear in his eye. He was lonely. But at least it was peaceful at dinner time. There was no mess and no more broken dishes. The four-year-old watched it all in silence.

One evening, the son noticed his little boy playing with some wood scraps on the floor. He asked the child sweetly, "What are you making?" The four-year-old looked up innocently and said, "Oh, I am making a little bowl for you to eat your food when I grow up."

Needless to say, the small boy's comment changed everything. His parents recognized the ultimate parenting principle: Children do what children see, good or bad. Years ago, I heard John Maxwell share about Sarah Edwards. The wife of the famous eighteenth-century clergyman Jonathan Edwards, she was passionate about investing in her children. She set aside time to develop leadership qualities in each of her kids—which took a large portion of her time. She had eleven children.

Author A. E. Winship wrote about Sarah Edwards, indicating "the way children turn out is always a reflection of their mother." Then, he chronicled the contributions that streamed from the Edwards family. Of the descendants that could be located, their family produced:

- 13 college presidents
- 65 professors
- 100 lawyers and a dean of a law school
- 30 judges
- 66 physicians and a dean of a medical school
- 80 holders of public office, including 3 U.S. senators, 3 mayors, 3 state governors, a U.S. treasury controller and a vice president of the United States

Winship pointed out that historians say much of the capacity and talent, intensity and character of the Edwards family is due to the modeling of Mrs. Edwards.[2]

4. It's Not the Quality or Quantity of Time We Spend, but the Quantity of Quality Time.

Notice what Moses said next: "You shall teach them diligently to your children . . ." (Deut. 6:7).

A big family debate during my lifetime revolves around quality time versus quantity time. Which is more important? I suppose I could argue for both. We need both quantity and quality time with our kids. Moses, however, seems to have a new angle on this issue. The issue isn't either/or. The issue is the amount of good quality time you get to experience meaningful conversation and relationship. It is the quantity of quality time you experience. This means you must welcome the teachable moments when they come and plan for them when they don't seem to be coming naturally.

Emma K. Halbert said, "Parents are prone to give their children everything except the one thing they need most. That is time. Time for listening, time for understanding, time for helping, and time for guiding. It sounds simple, but in reality, it is the most difficult and most sacrificial task of parenthood." One hundred years ago, parents spent 54 percent of their waking hours with their children. Today, parents spend 18 percent of their waking hours with them. Dr. Robert Blum is right when he says, "We call ourselves a family oriented society [but] we are not. We are a work-oriented society. Kids are left to their own devices." As parents, we need to get things straight. Our children need a large quantity of quality time if we expect them to embrace the values we are communicating. Where do we find it? Stephen Covey suggests the issue is not prioritizing our schedule but scheduling our priorities. Put it in the calendar now.

When parents and kids do have time together, it is often hurried and filled with noise. It is seldom what we could call "quality time." Kids spend eight more hours each week in school than they did in 1981. They do more household chores and accompany their parents on more errands. Participation in organized activities is up 50 percent since 1981. Obviously, this is not bad. We just have to determine if this is truly quality time together. If it is just noise and activity, we are teaching the wrong things. Weekly leisure time available between parents and kids dropped from 40 percent in 1981 to less than 25 percent today.[3] Let's make the most of it.

5. What's Worth Remembering Is Worth Repeating.

Finally, notice what Moses said in verse 7: "Talk of them when you sit in your house, when you walk by the way, when you lie down, and when you rise up."

One of our natural human weaknesses is forgetfulness. Even adults need to hear something multiple times before they'll retain it. Kids are no different, especially if it isn't something they deem relevant or desirable. Think about the times you've asked your child to do chores around the house. Did you have to bring it up more than once? If not, you are rare. I commend you as a parent.

Moses instructs his Hebrew neighbors to talk about important truths and principles in a variety of contexts. He suggests they bring them up over and over again. If it is worth remembering, it is worth repeating. What gets rewarded gets done. What gets repeated gets done. Consequently, my wife and I sat down and determined what the most important items were that we wanted our kids to embrace. We came up with a handful of them. Some of them change as our kids mature and master the principles. Until then, we repeat, repeat, repeat. I've discovered important principles will be remembered if we:

1. Shape them concisely. Be sure they are short and simple.

2. Share them constantly. Be sure they are communicated over and over.

3. Show them creatively. Be sure they are demonstrated in imaginative ways.

Have you ever noticed that things get taken for granted? Especially important things. This is why we must not assume our kids will naturally catch leadership values if we fail to talk about them regularly. According to a new study from Purdue University, unless the content of our values is articulated verbally, children may not have an accurate perception of what to believe or practice. Both modeling and talking about values are crucial. It is show and tell. The study found that kids catch values better when their relationship with both parents is good; when both parents share values; and when those values are repeated again and again. Wow. They just confirmed what Moses said four thousand years ago.

When my daughter, Bethany, was eight years old, I wanted to begin exposing her to great leaders. Although she didn't fully understand why, I took her to meetings to see great motivational speakers, I had her shake hands with great pastors and asked those pastors to pray for her, and I took her on trips to meet national leaders. In 1997, I took her to Washington, D.C., to meet several congressmen and senators. It was the National Day of Prayer, and I knew a number of them would assemble in the capitol building to discuss and pray for our nation. She got to meet several of them, including J. C. Watts, who spoke about the need to pray for our country. He repeated five requests for which we each could pray. Then, Bethany knelt down beside me to pray for our leaders in that great capital city. I knew the trip would be memorable for both of us, but frankly I didn't know if she would remember details. After all, she was only eight.

On the plane ride home, we talked about the different memorials and restaurants we visited. We talked about the pillow fight we had in the hotel and the cold cheeseburger we ate late at night. When our flight attendant brought us a snack, Bethany told me she wanted to pray before we ate. This was not uncommon. What struck me was—she remembered everything that Congressman J. C. Watts had asked us to pray for, and she covered them in her prayer on the plane.

Bethany had heard a fresh voice echo the things her mom and dad had shared at home. This time she got it. Likely, it was both the new voice and the repetition that helped her remember, but she got it. It had been a teachable moment for her in Washington, D.C. Now, I am on the look-out for those moments to share the leadership principles she needs to learn. In the next chapter, I'll let you in on the places where those moments happen on a daily basis.

Reflect and Respond

1. Have you summarized the priorities you want to teach your child?

2. How are you modeling the principles you wish them to learn?

3. Why do you think relationships have so much to do with a child's teachability?

10

DAILY OPPORTUNITIES TO MENTOR YOUR KIDS

*You cannot change your ancestors, but you can
do something about your descendants.*
—ANONYMOUS

NOT LONG AGO, I HEARD ABOUT A PASTOR who took a risky step. He was tired of seeing drug lords ruin his neighborhood and recruit his kids. He decided to do something radical and ask the drug dealers how they managed to be so successful in recruiting these young people and turning them to an empty, dangerous drug life.

The answer he received from the top drug pusher in the neighborhood was simple but piercing: "I'm there. You're not." When the pastor appeared shocked, he went on. "When these kids go to school in the morning—I'm there, you're not. When they hang out at the convenience store in the afternoon—I'm there, you're not. When they need someone to feel strong and tough and protected around—I'm there, you're not. I win, you lose."[1]

These words scream in the face of many parents. Millions of teenagers never get much time with an adult. In many cases, neither do pre-teens. The life of a parent can be overwhelming and time-consuming. We love our kids, but our days are full of demands. Today's parents are often overstressed, overworked, preoccupied, and sometimes just plain absent. Kids need adults who are present and awake. Step one is simple. They just need us to show up!

Although they'd never admit it, each day parents spend more time getting ready in the morning than they do getting their kids ready for life. When the children are gone, those same parents say things like, "I wish I'd spent more time with my son or daughter." I've never heard any of them say, "I wish I'd spent more time getting ready in the morning!" So, what do we do? Before it's too late, what can be done to daily invest in our children?

There is a huge nursery in Canada where thousands of trees and plants are grown. On the entrance wall is a big sign: "The best time to plant a tree is twenty-five years ago." In larger letters underneath, it says: "The second best time is today!"

Although you may feel you've lost precious time with your child, you still have today. The keys to making the most of today can be summarized in four terms:

1. **Show up** (your presence is half the battle).

2. **Wake up** (get on the same page with them mentally).

3. **Set up** (prepare for opportunities to pass on principles and truths).

4. **Speak up** (look for opportunities; don't let them pass you by when they come).

TIME IS AT A PREMIUM

Because the schedules of parents and schoolchildren today are so tight, good use must be made of every day. Kids are busier now than they have ever been. They feel pressure to perform both in school and in the myriad of activities available afterward. There is pressure to "make the grade, make the team, make the money." The pendulum has swung again to an extreme, where our educators are demanding more from students. High-school principal Marilyn Cook said, "There's pressure to achieve in everything. It can make the brightest kid in the world feel inadequate." My daughter has been in tears more than once because she has so much homework. She must work on it from the moment she gets home from school to the moment she goes to bed at night with a short break at dinnertime. Obviously, this gives us little time to actually behave as a family! You may feel this same stress. School consumes children's time and energy and has more control over their waking hours than Mom and Dad.

All of this has left me determined to make the most of my time with my kids. If I'm going to assume the primary responsibility to nurture the leader in my children, I must capitalize on the opportunities that arise each day to do so. I believe Charles Richards was right when he said, "Don't be fooled by the calendar. There are only as many days in the year as we make use of. One person gets a week's value out of a year while another person gets a year's value out of a week."

Four Optimal Opportunities in Your Day

In the last chapter, we chatted about what Moses taught us about teaching our kids. In this chapter, I want to return to his passage from the book of Deuteronomy and consider it in greater detail. If we look closely at Deuteronomy 6:7, we discover something very interesting. Moses suggested four good opportunities for parents to discuss truth with their children. Look with me at the passage again:

> You shall teach [these truths] diligently to your children, and shall talk
> of them when you sit in your house, when you walk by the way, when you
> lie down, and when you rise up.

Of course! All of a sudden, it made sense. My friend Reggie Joiner pointed out that these four junctions are opportunities for parents to invest in their kids every day: mealtime, travel time, bedtime, and morning time.

Instead of merely reacting to circumstances and hoping some teachable moment arises, we can predict the daily opportunities we will get even a few minutes with our kids—and make the most of them.

1. Mealtime.

One of my favorite times of the day is mealtime. (And it's not just because I love food!) It's because in our home, we push the pause button in our hectic day and try to sit down together as a family. The meal is simply a good excuse to slow down, to be real, and to connect. For centuries the Hebrew culture saw mealtimes as natural times to communicate, to debrief the lessons the kids got from their tutor, to laugh together, and to build relationships. I agree. Some of my fondest memories of growing up are of my parents and two sisters talking around the dinner table during a meal. I still remember particular statements made at dinner that have stuck with me and guided my thinking as an adult. Those statements weren't always directed toward me either. They were made between adults.

In fact, my dad spoke to me about these times just a few months ago. He challenged me to try to remember as many conversations as I could from my boyhood. I scribbled down a dozen. Then, he said, "I'm guessing that many of those statements you remember were things said between your mother and me, weren't they?" Sure enough, he was right. All but one of them were conversations between Mom and Dad.

You see, if you really want to get your kids' attention and teach them something, allow them to get in earshot of a conversation between adults. Those ears always perk up. My dad, aware of the eavesdropping, would teach us kids as he and Mom conversed. My dad even said to me recently, "The problem with America is that we aren't eating supper together." Meals are priceless learning centers. Meals are a sacrament. Truth is shared naturally over meals. A table full of food gives us a safe place to think out loud. I am happy to report many Americans are beginning to rediscover this reality. Mary Pipher, author of *Reviving Ophelia*, wrote, "Churches are actually having family meals classes, where they have a whole generation of young parents who never had family meals themselves. They don't know how to do it. And they want to."[2]

The mealtime allows you to fill the role of a teacher. My wife and I have learned that we do best when we choose one character quality or one principle per month and talk about it at as many mealtimes as possible. Our kids expect a purposeful discussion. I will write down four or five questions I want my kids to interact over and share their thoughts. For instance, last month we interacted about the leadership skill of self-discipline. We talked about movies that portray discipline; books we've read that contain a character who had discipline or failed to have it in their life; how we see it demonstrated in each other's life; and how we can better build it into our own. Another evening, we watched the news as we ate. I asked my kids to choose a crisis and talk about it. Then I asked what they might do if they were in charge of solving that problem. It was a marvelous leadership discussion. We have found it is realistic to have between one and three of these discussions per week. We keep a card on our kitchen table to remind us of each month's subject. This month we are discussing generosity.

One mother practiced this same exercise with her son, Jamie. He was prone to be selfish, as many nine-year-olds are. They talked for an entire week about generosity and how wonderful it is to possess a generous spirit with others. It was February and Valentine's Day was approaching. Jamie got an idea. He could show generosity to his classmates by personally creating a valentine card for each of them. His mom thought it was a great idea but was hesitant. She feared he might be disappointed if his friends did not return the gesture. She didn't want him to be disappointed. The next day, she called his teacher to see if they planned to exchange valentine cards. "No, we are not taking time for that this year," was her reply. It made no difference to Jamie. He was determined to stick with his idea. His only concern was making sure he finished them all. He stayed up late to make twenty-four cards that night.

The next day, Jamie's mom had made cookies as a consolation prize for him. She knew how disappointed he became when friends didn't return an act of kindness. As Jamie walked through the door, her heart sank. She knew her fears were realized. He was mumbling, "Not one. Not one!" She grabbed the cookies and ran to meet him at the garage door.

Then, she heard him continue. "I didn't forget one valentine! I didn't leave out one friend!" Obviously, Jamie learned his first lesson in generosity. His focus had changed from himself to others, and it all began at mealtime.

Another mom began discussing racial equality with her middle-school-aged kids. Their school had students from a variety of nationalities, and prejudice had become an issue. When her daughter asked if everyone really was equal, she decided to turn mealtime into a classroom. She grabbed three apples out of the refrigerator, a red one, a yellow one, and a green one. The family discussed how different the colors were. Then, she peeled the skin off and scrambled the order of the apples. The kids could not tell which was the red, the yellow, or the green one. Then, she had them taste each one. All of them were delicious. They got the point.

2. Travel Time.

Moses also spoke of teaching kids as we travel along the road. What a novel idea. Time in the car or minivan with our kids is often wasted. We find ways to entertain ourselves but seldom use it to enhance growth. Why not stay focused on a character value or a leadership skill and talk about it in a creative way? Drive time is a wonderful time for educational conversation because you are cooped up together; no one is going anywhere until you arrive at your destination; distractions are relatively low; and most of the family is looking for ways to avoid being bored. Sometimes I will bring a tape with me that we can listen to together to spark discussion. Frequently, we do something as simple as listen to a song on a CD and talk about the meaning of the lyrics. We interpret what the band was really saying and decide whether or not we agree with its values. If we see an accident, we stop and pray for the people or even give assistance. If help is already there, we may discuss the question: If I was in charge of helping the people in that car accident, what would I do? All kinds of leadership situations arise and can be discussed in the car.

The travel time opportunity allows you to fill the role of a friend to your children. It's a casual and safe environment. It is an even more informal talk time than mealtime. We can teach them to interpret life. Travel time provides the space to say things that might need to be said but would be more difficult in a more distracting environment. For example, my friend George spoke to me about how demanding he was when his kids were younger. He set high standards and expectations. Kim, his sixteen-year-old daughter, began to resent it. She grew bitter toward him when she would fail to meet his standards. (Bitterness almost always turns to rebellion, unless the parents can cut it off.) George knew he had to do something. He wanted to reconnect with Kim and decided to set the example and take initiative. He asked if she would drive him to a meeting he had two hours away. She didn't want to and told her mom: "All he's going to do is preach, preach, preach to me!" Her mother urged her to go, and she finally agreed reluctantly.

On the way, the first five miles were silent, and George's mouth became dry and his hands started to sweat. He wasn't sure how to begin talking to her. There was so much he wanted to say, but he could tell she wasn't in any mood to hear it, as she stared straight ahead. Finally, George cleared his throat and softly said, "Kim, I need you to do me a favor."

"What?" she asked begrudgingly.

"I need you to forgive me." He paused. "I have been so demanding on you, and I know I have discouraged you with my high standards. I never meant to do that. Do you think you could forgive me?"

One large tear began to stream down Kim's cheek. She couldn't take her eyes off the road, but for the first time in months, she was ready to talk. "I forgive you, Daddy."

His request opened up a door of conversation that lasted the entire trip. Further, that road trip was the breakthrough in their relationship. Both George and Kim became teachable again.

Sometimes, our family plays games in the car, as I'm sure your family has. I will often make them age-appropriate learning games for my kids. For example, you might want to play a leadership game I call: "change the navigator." When you are at a place where any of two or more routes would be satisfactory, let your child be the navigator. If it is a long road trip, show them a map, and discuss the relative advantages of each route. Then, let them choose. Don't agree or disagree. Let them guide the family along the way. You'll be amazed at the discussions that will arise from this exercise. (Pssst. One more thing. Be sure you have plenty of time to get there!)

We've played another game when we drive through a new town—we imagine what it would be like to live there. We ask each other: How would it be different from where we live now? What kinds of problems do kids have here? How would you feel if you learned we had to move in one month? What would you do to prepare to move? What kind of house would you want to live in? How would you build new friendships?

Sometimes, we just ask trivia questions relevant to our trip. What was the waitress's name in the restaurant where we just ate? (This gets them thinking about the importance of names and people.) Why was Mom so upset last Monday? Or, what was the lesson we learned from that movie we saw last weekend?

3. Bedtime.

The most intimate conversations in our house happen at bedtime. For some reason, my kids become more vulnerable and transparent at bedtime than during the day. They are almost always ready to talk. (It's probably a stall tactic!)

The bedtime opportunity allows you to build intimacy and to fill the role of a counselor to your children. At my house, I still tuck my kids into bed when I am home. Like many families, we usually have a story time and a prayer time. The power of story comes through so loudly at bedtime. I always tell a story that teaches a leadership value to my kids. I would rather my kids learn through stories than tragic experiences, although I believe some lessons are only grasped through real-life struggles. Stories go over well and are *remembered* because they capture a child's imagination. The younger your kids are, the more concretely they think. This means they require a story or example to learn a concept. Abstract thinking (where their mind can think in concepts) doesn't happen until their teen years. Even then, I still try to give them a "point" for their head and a "picture" for their heart. When choosing a story, ask yourself:

1. Is there a story from my past that illustrates this truth I want them to learn?

---

2. Is there a story from their world that illustrates this truth I want them to learn?

3. Is there a story from past or current events that illustrates this truth I want them to learn?

I have discovered that different kinds of stories have different levels of impact. For instance, the depth of impact usually follows this sequence:

a. Personal and true stories—tales that come from my own experience are best

b. Daily life and true stories—stories that come from their own day-to-day world

c. Common and true stories—stories that are common knowledge to everyone

d. Historical and true stories—pages from the annals of history

e. Fiction—stories that are not true but interesting

I'll never forget hearing about one mom who witnessed the power of a story with her son, Willard. Each night, Willard would hear his mom talk about possessing a good heart, a heart that longed to generously help others. She would literally teach her son through stories. At school, Willard tended to be a loner. He wasn't social and didn't build friendships easily. He was often silent and indifferent. Perhaps his mom sensed this and was trying to help him grow. In December, his teacher, Mr. Collins, reported that the school planned to participate in an annual Christmas collection for needy families. Mr. Collins encouraged the kids to look beyond their own needs and think of others during the Christmas season. The next morning, the class was to bring in something for the collection. Needless to say, it was disappointing when almost every student forgot to bring something. That is, except for Willard. He strolled up to his teacher's desk and dropped in two quarters. "I don't need no milk for lunch," he mumbled. For a moment, he smiled, then returned to his desk.

Later, Mr. Collins took the meager contribution to the principal. He mentioned Willard's gift and told him how encouraged he was by it, despite the failure of the rest of the class to show any generosity. "I think Willard is getting it!" he said. The principal smiled in agreement, then told the teacher that he needed to see something. He reached for the list of the poor families they would be serving in the community. Willard's family was at the top of the list.[3]

Willard learned that leadership has little to do with what you've got in your wallet and everything to do with what you've got between your ears. Perspective often comes from Mom at bedtime. My son, Jonathan, had a tough day recently, and he couldn't shake a bad attitude. Only eight, but he expressed a lifetime of utter disappointment when he wrote a note and attached it to my door at home:

"This is the baddest day of Jonathan's life. P.S. I hope your day is better than Jonathan's."

He couldn't see anything good coming from this rotten day. I knew I had to do something, so that night I decided to put my artistic talents to the test. I grabbed a piece of paper and asked him to draw a squiggly line on it—one line that represented his crooked day. He did. His line went all over. Then, I took the pencil and began to make a cartoon out of it. Fortunately, my plan and my picture turned out great. Then I talked to him about how we need to trust God to make something good come out of every bad or confusing situation. Bedtime redeemed the entire day for him. He still has the little cartoon picture we drew that night.

As you prepare for bedtime, you might consider doing a story or exercise on the principle or character quality you discussed at mealtime. Consistency is key for kids of all ages. Consistency in your discipline, your love, and your discussion. I mentioned earlier I sometimes play a little game called "making sense of your day." In this game, I let my kids talk about events or people in their day that confused or upset them and then interpret what happened and help them gain perspective. I take advantage of the moments they are most ready for me to be their counselor.

4. Morning Time.

Moses listed "rising up" as the final opportunity we have each day with our kids. I try to take a few minutes with my kids before they start their day to encourage and to motivate them. At morning time, they need me to fill the role of both a coach and a cheerleader. I attempt to get them excited about the new day and its opportunities. I use lots and lots of humor. I think it's important to laugh early, as it sets a tone for the day. It begins with the moment we wake them up, to the time they brush their teeth, to the time at the breakfast table. I may run into their room with a towel around me like a superhero cape and challenge them to attack the day. I may recite a ridiculous poem or even sing a song. (They smile as they tell me they hate it!)

Then, I move into a few minutes of encouragement. Pam and I want them to leave the house secure in their parents' love for them, believing they can make a difference to others and feeling bold enough to try. You might say, every morning I am shaping their self-esteem. I believe if a child has a healthy self-esteem, chances are high they will lead others. I often give them one assignment to take on during the day, such as: Find one person who needs encouragement and give it to him. Or, help your teacher today before the bell rings for lunch. Or, show your friends what responsibility looks like sometime during the day.

One dad did this in a creative way, as related in *Chicken Soup for the Preteen Soul.* He had two tickets to a big basketball game in town. It was the quarterfinals, and all three of his kids wanted desperately to go with him. The game was sold out, so there was no chance of getting any more tickets. He had to make a choice.

He spoke with all three of his kids, and they all lobbied for why they should be the one who went with him to the game. He finally concluded he would find some way to give the ticket to the most deserving of the three of them. The next morning, the dad tried to motivate them to get busy on their Saturday chores. The two sons continued to play ball outside, but the daughter began her chores. When she finally had put the last bit of trash in the wastebasket and reached down to take the full plastic bag out, she noticed an envelope taped to the top of the wastebasket that read: "Congratulations!" Inside were the two tickets. Dad had found a way for his kids to learn a lesson in responsibility and earn their own rewards.[4]

As my wife and I see our kids off, we sometimes like to put notes in their backpacks. These are simply reminders of our love and belief in them. Encouragement. Motivation. Support. The notes might communicate that we noticed something good they did the day before. It might be a written prayer for them to do well on their afternoon math test. It might contain a great quote. Or, it might just be a love note.

TIME IN A BOTTLE?

I'm convinced, as a parent, that I must take advantage of these natural junctions I have with my kids each day. I want to look forward to a future filled with reward, not regret. I want to know I seized every moment I could to invest in them.

You may remember pop musician Jim Croce, from the 1970s. He wrote a popular song, "Time in a Bottle," in which he said he wanted to store time in a bottle. When he needed some time for his family, he could uncork the bottle and take some time out. When he needed some time for his friends, he could uncork the bottle and take some time out. The song was about saving up extra time to use it when he needed it.

Less than twelve months from the day he recorded that song, he was killed in a plane crash. All of his time was gone. Even if he'd been able to bottle up time, that bottle would have been smashed in the wreckage. We can't save time like we do money—we always spend it on something. What are you spending yours on?

ONE THOUSAND MARBLES

I heard about a man who learned this lesson before it was too late. He wrote:

A few weeks ago, I was shuffling toward my basement with a steaming cup of coffee in one hand and a newspaper in the other. What began as a typical Saturday morning turned into one of those lessons that life seems to hand you from time to time.

I turned up the dial on the phone portion of my ham radio in order to listen to a Saturday morning swap net. I came across an elderly-sounding man, who was telling someone about a theory he had—something about a thousand marbles. I stopped to listen. He said, "Well, Tom, it sure sounds like you're busy with your job. I'm sure they pay you well, but it's a shame you have to be away from your family so much. Too bad you missed your daughter's dance recital." There was a pause. Obviously, Tom had no rebuttal. "Let me tell you something, Tom . . . something that has helped me keep a good perspective on my own priorities. I call it my theory of a thousand marbles.

"You see, I sat down one day and did a little arithmetic. The average person lives about seventy-five years. Now then, I multiplied 75 times 52 and came up with 3,900, which is the number of Saturdays the average person has in their entire lifetime. Now stick with me, Tom, I'm getting to the important part.

"It took me until I was fifty-five years old to think about this in any detail . . . and by that time I had lived over 2,800 Saturdays. I got to thinking that if I lived to be seventy-five, I had about a thousand Saturdays left to enjoy. So, I went to a toy store and bought up every single marble they had. In fact, I had to go to three stores to round up a thousand marbles. I took them home and put them inside a large plastic container. Every Saturday since then, I have taken one marble out and thrown it away. I found that by watching the marbles diminish, I focused more on the really important things in life. There is nothing like watching your time here on this earth run out to help get your priorities straight.

"Now, let me tell you one last thing before I sign off and take my lovely wife to breakfast. This morning, I took the very last marble out of the container. I figure if I make it until next Saturday, then I have been given a little extra time. And, the one thing we can all use is a little more time. It was nice to meet you, Tom. I hope you get more time with your family."

Then . . . he signed off. You could have heard a pin drop when this guy signed off. I guess he gave us all a lot to think about. I planned to get some work done on my antenna, then finish my e-mails from the office . . . but decided to change my plans. Instead, I went upstairs and woke my wife up with a kiss.

"C'mon, honey. I'm taking you and the kids to breakfast."

"What brought this on?" she asked with a smile.

"Oh, nothing special. It's just been a long time since we spent a Saturday together with the kids.

"By the way, can we stop by a toy store while we are out? I need to buy some marbles."

Reflect and Respond

1. What are some topics you'd like to talk about with your kids?

2. How could you incorporate them into these four daily junctions?

3. When will you start?

11

CREATING MEMORIES, CAPITALIZING ON MOMENTS, CONSUMING MATERIALS

Before I got married, I had six theories on raising kids. Now, I have six kids and no theories.
—LORD ROCHESTER, 1675

GARY WAS RUNNING OUT OF IDEAS TO TEACH his kids how to keep a good attitude. Perhaps they were spoiled—they did get what they wanted most of the time. Perhaps he needed to remind them how good they had it, living in San Diego, California. Perhaps they just needed to learn how to stay positive when things didn't go their way. Whatever it was, he was weary of their whining over the slightest change in plans. They got so negative they actually began expecting the worst in situations. His lectures didn't seem to work. His discipline didn't seem to work. He needed some creative method for drilling in how good can come from bad situations, if they would only look at the bright side of things.

Then, it hit him. After a discussion with his wife, he announced to the kids that they would take a little vacation the following month. They were going to drive to Texas, to visit relatives and swim in their pool. The kids were elated at the news. Gary waited until a week before the trip—then announced that he wouldn't be able to make the trip. They would have to go without him. He needed to stay home and work on a project at the office.

The kids reacted just as he suspected they would. They began to complain about how the vacation would be ruined if he couldn't go with them. He insisted, however, that they look at the bright side of things. They would still get to go to see their cousins and swim in their big pool. Gary wouldn't let them get up from the conversation until they promised to see the good in a less-than-optimal situation. Reluctantly, they agreed to stop grumbling and smile.

Little did they know what Dad had up his sleeve. As Mom and the kids pulled out of the driveway on their excursion, Dad hurried to the airport to fly to Phoenix. As Mom and the kids drove along Interstate 8 going eastward across Arizona, they got the shock of their life. Glancing out their window, they saw Dad—hitchhiking on the freeway! The kids screamed at their mother to stop the car. Grinning from ear to ear, Mom stopped to pick up Dad. All of them laughed at the situation, and Gary got the chance of a lifetime to talk about surprises and attitude. You never know what's around the next bend—so you gotta keep an open mind and open eyes.

Needless to say, Gary's creativity was a hit. That vacation has lingered in their minds for years. He had created a memory and taught his kids a lesson at the same time. This is the kind of mentoring I not only admire but want to emulate in my home. I believe if we're going to mentor our kids in leadership, we will deepen our impact if we learn to create memories and capture moments.

Obviously, this will require us to live with our antennas up. Investing in our kids must become a priority in our minds, pocketbooks, and calendars. It's the easiest thing to say, "I just don't have what it takes to be creative. I'm spent when I finally get home." Author Wayne Muller wrote: "'I'm so busy.' We say this to one another with no small degree of pride, as if our exhaustion were a trophy, our ability to withstand stress a mark of real character. The busier we are the more important we seem to ourselves, and we imagine to others. To be unavailable to our friends and family, to be unable to find time for the sunset, to whiz through our obligations without time for a single, mindful breath, this has become the model of a successful life."[1] Is it really?

I recognize that today's kids and parents are busy. I got to thinking, however, about the opportunity I had, if I would only seize the moment. I figured our church had our kids for about 1 percent of the time. The school had them about 18 percent of the time. I had them 81 percent of the time. I had to make the most of my prospects! I soon discovered this would mean focusing on three areas: creating memories, capitalizing on moments, and consuming materials.

CREATING MEMORIES

The term "creating memories" is not new. It became popular some twenty years ago. We create memories by deliberately setting up environments that will generate special experiences. It may be a unique vacation, like Gary planned for his family. It may be a field trip and discussion on a specific issue, or it might even be a creative learning event at home. I remember a number of such times when I was growing up. One of the reasons I have taken my kids to our nation's capital to talk about great leaders in our history is because I took a special trip to that city when I was in fifth grade. I can recall specific moments, what I saw, what I wore, what I ate, and the people I met. It is uncanny how it stuck in my mind.

A Photographer

The word picture I keep in my mind is a photographer. When we create memories, we're like a photographer setting up just the right scene and capturing it on film. In our case, we are capturing it in the minds of our kids.

Think back to your childhood. Can you remember any special moments? Don't they linger in your mind like a snapshot? To be sure, if you don't think of them often, they can fade just like an old picture, but they usually stick with us like a full-color photo. What's more, they often dictate the way we think and feel. We'll even make decisions based on the photographs we carry in our minds. A case in point is the huge market right now for nostalgia among baby boomers. From baseball card collections, to old TV shows, to comic books, to Batman and other super heroes—we have witnessed an enormous amount of spending because adults are trying to recapture moments from their past. They have an old photograph in their minds, and they want to freshen it up.

Obviously, I believe we can use this to teach leadership. I already mentioned our family trip to Washington, D.C. It was a memorable trip for my kids, Bethany and Jonathan. When we'd stop for a meal, we would talk about the memorials we had seen, such as the Lincoln, Roosevelt, Washington, and Vietnam memorials and monuments. We would talk about the ultimate contribution those leaders made. We would talk about their personal lives, their strengths, their weaknesses,, and why they did what they did. We would then pretend to be in their shoes and ask: What would I have done if I were the leader back then? I hear my children talk about the trip years afterward.

Temple Year

Bethany turned twelve last year. I believe this is a significant year for kids. In the Jewish culture, this is the year when young boys experience their bar mitzvah. In ancient Israel, twelve-year-old boys would be taken to the Temple as a rite of passage into manhood. In America, we don't have too many events that mark the passage from childhood into adulthood. The closest we come is obtaining a driver's license or a high school graduation ceremony. Because I feel this year is a special one, I determined to create a memory during my kids' twelfth year. I let my daughter choose a place she wanted to visit, and I would take her there for some special father-daughter time. She scared me as she thought about various places she wanted to go. She talked about going to Canada to ride a fast train, New York to experience the big city, Paris (gulp!) to see the Eiffel Tower, and Orlando, Florida. She finally decided to go to Orlando—because there were so many fun things to do there. And we did have fun. We laughed until we hurt as we visited Disney World and other parks. The fun times really prepared us for some meaningful sharing times, because it was a safe place to talk. At night, we sat down and talked about her future, her struggles, her temptations, her dreams, her weaknesses, her friends, her fears, and what her mom and I could do to help her grow. I just posed questions and let her talk. Some of my questions for her were:

- What's the toughest thing about being a twelve-year-old?
- What is your biggest temptation? (She won't let me tell you her response!)
- If you could change one thing about yourself, what would it be?
- What do you struggle with most regarding your faith?
- Are you tempted with sex yet?
- What are your thoughts about the future?
- What do you look for most in a friend? In a boyfriend?
- What's the scariest thought about growing up?
- What gifts do you believe God has given you?
- How can I help you grow?

Because I believe leadership is about serving others, our family feeds the homeless in downtown Atlanta at Safehouse Outreach. It has been good to see my children don gloves and serve hot plates to those who own one set of clothes and smell like they haven't washed them for days. I love seeing them set aside some of their money to give to charities and causes that help those in need. I love it when they take initiative and want to stop to help someone who needs it, as we walk or drive in our community. I love watching them as they visit another culture and see people in a developing nation grapple with just getting enough food, enough clothes, and enough shelter. I believe their heart is being shaped by these experiences. I am hopeful that Pam and I are creating memories.

I also want to create memories surrounding their gift areas. Jonathan loves art. Consequently, we have taken him to places where he can be exposed to great artists and artwork. By the time he was seven he had visited a Norman Rockwell exhibit to admire his work and art museums in three cities to explore the work of his favorite artist, Dr. Seuss. Bethany loves acting and music. Pam and I have taken her to Broadway shows such as *Phantom of the Opera, Beauty and the Beast,* and others. My goal is not to push them in any one direction but to foster the discovery of their own talent and passion. They will naturally lead in their gift areas.

Author Ron Blue told me how he took his sixteen-year-old daughter Denise on what was supposed to be an exciting father-daughter trip. She loved basketball, so Ron had purchased tickets to the NCAA basketball tournament that year. Unfortunately, the conversation didn't flow too well. Ron suggested ideas for activities all day, but Denise wasn't talking much. She was at a stage where she didn't have much to say. He told me he could hardly wait to get home. The trip felt long, because they just didn't connect. Or, did they? Years later, Denise told her husband: "That weekend with my dad was the most significant one of my life."

Creating memories doesn't always have to include a trip and spending a lot of money. Leadership can be taught in innovative ways right around the home. One dad I know wanted to teach his kids the value of believing in a cause. He wanted to help them see that belief sometimes costs you something—that achieving goals involves sacrifice. So he and his kids read about the sacrifices many made during World War Two. Not only did Americans grow victory gardens, but many Europeans helped those being persecuted by Hitler and the Nazis. Since his kids were old enough to appreciate some on-the-edge creativity, he got creative. After their reading, he and his kids reenacted a rescue. He turned the lights down, put on a CD, and played sounds of bombs blowing up. Then, they climbed into the crawl space of their house with flashlights to hide. While in the tight crawl space under their floor, they had some powerful conversation about how it felt to believe in something so strongly. What was worth this kind of action?

CAPITALIZING ON MOMENTS

Most parents feel they aren't very good at capitalizing on teachable moments. It is common for us to get caught up in our agenda and miss the moments when life becomes a classroom; those times when we can play off of something that occurs during the day and make it a learning time. Creating memories is proactive; capitalizing on them is reactive. It means staying alert to those serendipitous events that are unplanned but might serve as a great teaching tool for your kids. I have noticed when I do this the learning is often more memorable for my kids. Spontaneous events spark unique opportunities.

The Quarterback

This role can be likened to a quarterback in a college football game. Have you noticed that the quarterback position is a combination of planning and spontaneity? When a quarterback meets in the huddle with his team, he must call a play. However, his plays change based on an assortment of factors: the clock, his position on the field, the talent in his huddle, the down, and the amount of yards he must gain for a first down. Then, when he gets to the line of scrimmage, he must read the defense. If the opposing team is doing something unusual, the quarterback may call an "audible." He'll change his plans because the opposition has shifted. The goal is always the same. The plays change based on a variety of dynamics. He is always planning and responding to his circumstances. He is moving toward the end zone. He doesn't stay in the huddle because that's where things are safe and predictable! He will do whatever it takes to score.

For us as parents, scoring means raising our kids to reach their potential. So, we must play off the events that happen and turn them into learning times. Dan Clark wrote about such a moment for him as a young teenager in *A Second Helping of Chicken Soup for the Soul.* His dad took him to the circus one Saturday. Standing in the ticket line, he noticed a large family in front of them. He could tell they were poor. Their clothes were old, probably secondhand. The six kids acted like this was the first time they'd ever been to the circus. Unfortunately, when the family reached the clerk and heard the price of the tickets, the poor father didn't have enough money. But how was he going to tell his six expectant kids that they couldn't go to the circus?

Dan said that his dad quickly surmised what was happening. He reached into his pocket and pulled out a $20 bill and dropped it on the ground. Then, he leaned over and picked it up and said to the man, "Excuse me, sir, but I think this fell out of your pocket." The man had a tear in his eye as he responded, "Thank you, sir, thank you! You don't know what this means to my family." Dan and his father didn't get to go to the circus that day, but he said he didn't go without. He had watched his father model generosity and teach him a lesson in it without trying.[2] Can you imagine the conversation the two of them had on the way home? Talk about a learning moment.

There are four methods we can use to mentor our kids in leadership. Each of them allows us to capitalize on moments with them. The first method is *accidental mentoring*. This is where opportunities to teach occur and we don't even realize it. A friend of mine remembers learning from his dad growing up. He would watch his dad interact with a group of men. Whenever someone told an off-color joke, his dad would never join in. Instead, he would politely steer the conversation to higher ground. It made a deep impression on my friend.

A second method is *mentoring moments*. This is where we can take advantage of a learning opportunity during the day. My wife had just returned from the grocery store with our kids last Monday. When they arrived home, she realized they got home with an item they didn't pay for. What did she do? In the face of a hectic day, my wife hopped back in the van with our kids and returned to the store to pay for it. The kids watched as the clerk raved over her honesty. The employees couldn't believe it. The manager thanked her. It was a mentoring moment for our kids.

A third method is *mentoring events*. Kids love events, so why not plan on them? We take our kids to big events, whether they are movies or plays or even watching a special TV program, then we debrief them when they're over. We will teach leadership and character principles off of them. I have put together a videocassette of great movies that contain leadership scenes in them—movies like *Braveheart, Glory, Simon Birch, The Patriot, Stand and Deliver, Mr. Holland's Opus, Liar Liar, Patch Adams*, and others. I show them to my kids and talk about them as they grow old enough to understand them. Other events may include taking them to hear great speakers, then asking what they understood from their message.

A fourth method is *scheduled mentoring*. This happens in our home on date nights. I try to take my two kids on one-on-one dates each month. We don't spend a lot of money, but we have some good conversation. I often let them set the agenda. I plan to ask questions and listen. I will take this time to praise them for the good things I've noticed in their life and behavior or challenge them when they've done wrong. I let them make the decisions that night—then we talk about how and why they arrived at those choices. This is all part of leadership development!

My friends, Andy and Sandra, want their kids to learn self-leadership first. When they are home, they will purposefully have their kids work out their sibling conflict among themselves. This way, they see the necessity of negotiation, and they learn the art of giving and receiving. They also want their kids to grow in relation to others. So, they place their children in situations that will stretch them; places where they are slightly over their head. For instance, their oldest son played on a basketball team. Andy helped coach it and asked his son to be a team captain in an inter-squad game. His son, Andrew, was a much less skilled player than the other team captain. So this was a challenge for Andrew. What a joy it was for my friend to see his son rise to the occasion and begin to give direction to his teammates that night. On their way home, they talked about how young Andrew felt and why he had made the choices he made. Learning moments.

Another dad I know found a mentoring moment after his son's basketball practice. His son worked hard and had made the school team as a freshman. He beat out three dozen other students for the fifteenth spot on the team. Because he was young and inexperienced, however, he spent most of his time on the bench. One night after practice, the freshman came home and announced he was going to quit the team. He would try out another year when he could get more playing time. His dad had other thoughts. He told his son: "Think about what you are doing. There are thirty-six guys that you beat out to get on this team. You are not going to quit because you took the spot they would have taken. This is called responsibility." Needless to say, it was a teachable moment.

CONSUMING MATERIALS

When I refer to "consuming materials," I am speaking of finding resources for your children to read, watch, or play that will help them understand leadership. These will be books, magazines, videos, computer games, or even video games that they will enjoy playing and may just enjoy talking about afterward. For instance, I pay my children $5 for each biography they read. They get paid to do the chores around the house—why not for reading about a great leader who might indirectly mentor them? Once they read the book, they must give me a verbal or written report of two things they learned from it.

One dad I know has his kids watch TV commercials just to discuss them afterward. I'm sure you have noticed a large amount of television commercials make outrageous claims. Others appeal to the viewers' feelings without explaining the benefits of the product. Many ads seem to promise happiness if only you buy their product. Even young kids are smart enough to detect dishonest or misguided ads. My friend will debrief the logic and influence of each commercial. He will even have his kids talk back to the set and argue with the TV announcer! They are learning how to consume and think critically about persuasion.

Whether it's books, TV, magazines, or videos—I suggest you find tools your kids can consume to help them think and act and become more like a leader.

Pitchers of Water

Reggie Joiner compares our task to pitchers of water. Water is a staple. Civilizations have always needed it. Cities are built beside rivers because of the timeless need for water. However, the containers or pitchers different civilizations use have changed over the years. The ancient Egyptian culture used pitchers that look very different from those used in twentieth-century America. It doesn't matter, though, because the containers simply carry the water. The water is still the same.

If we step back at an arm's length, we can see that cultures and generations are much like pitchers of water. The water is the timeless truths and principles we want to pass on to the next generation—namely, our children. Water will always be carried in some kind of pitcher, so we must find pitchers to suit our kids' generations and use them! This may mean they don't latch on to the same books that impacted us or like the same movies we do. That's OK because movies and books are only "pitchers." The key is to get past the containers and focus on getting the "water" to our kids in a pitcher they will drink from. The principles are timeless; the methods or tools will come and go.

So, what are some pitchers your kids will drink from? When I ask that question, the answers are revealing to my wife and me. For instance, here are some of the best ways for me to get my kids to consume leadership principles:

1. Let them pick out a biography to read. Pay them $5 to read it and report on the leadership principles they learn from it.

2. Bring up a leadership principle and have them act it out. It may be a story they know. Give them a part in a little drama to participate in, then talk about it afterward.

3. Take them to a leadership or personal growth conference, when they are old enough to understand it. Share with them the principles *you* learned at the conference, then ask them what they learned.

4. Purchase tapes, videos, and CDs that include leadership or character truths on them. They may be music CDs. Discuss the words and their meaning.

5. If you have a middle schooler, you may want to purchase age-appropriate books or workbooks for them. For instance, I like the Power Pak series that includes, "Leading from Your Locker," "Leading on Your Sports Team," "Leading in Your Youth Group," and "Leading Your Friends," from Tommy Nelson Publishers.

6. Have your child read the newspaper and pick a story to talk about. Ask them: Is there a problem to be solved? Is there a solution that

might work? What would they do if they were asked to be the leader to solve the problem?

7. Determine a leadership case study you want to talk about with your child. Entice them to talk by confiding in them your own need for growth. Mona Leger-Chutz and Bill Beausay suggest if we have teenagers, we should start with statements such as:

- "I have a secret to share with you . . . "

- "I'm embarrassed, but there's something I have to admit to you . . . "

- "What I'm about to say will blow you away; are you sure you can handle it?"

- "This is probably going to surprise you about me . . . "

- "I don't know how to tell you this . . . "

In her provocative article, "You Can Raise Your Child's IQ," Maya Pines challenges parents to help raise their children's intelligence "in the crucial early years when it is most malleable." I found her research very interesting. She claims that three things must be accomplished in the home in order to help raise a child's IQ. These are: "stimulation in infancy, early language activities, and preparation for reading." This gives me all the more incentive to encourage my kids to do more than "veg" in front of the TV watching mindless programs but to read and talk to discover the necessary principles they need for life.[3]

One of the results of this input is a healthy self-esteem. Despite what television networks tell us, children are affected by what they feed their minds. Potential can go untapped simply because a child feels unworthy to accomplish something significant. Just ask Victor. He was five years old when his family emigrated from Russia to the U.S. Because he was old enough to start kindergarten, his parents put him in school but with no culture or language preparation. Within a few months, his classmates had him labeled as stupid. By second grade, his teachers had him in remedial groups. Things just grew worse through middle school. Finally, in high school, a student pulled him aside and said, "Victor, you're not keeping up. Instead of holding the rest of our class back, why don't you just drop out of school and take a job that doesn't require you to be smart? Maybe you can make ends meet."

Victor decided to do just that. He dropped out of school at age sixteen and worked several jobs for the next fourteen years. At age thirty, something dramatic happened—Victor took an IQ test. He couldn't believe the results. His IQ was 161. He was a genius! His mind was the best-kept secret in his school for twenty-five years! From the moment of that discovery, his life was revolutionized.

Here's my point. Did Victor suddenly get smart at thirty years of age? Of course not. It was in him all the time. What changed was the way he saw himself. Instead of waking up in the morning, looking in the mirror, and seeing an idiot, he saw a genius. He finally had some good input.

The good news is, this story has a happy ending. Victor did discover his potential. The bad news is, much of his life was wasted due to faulty input. I don't know about you, but when my kids look in the mirror, I want them to see what's really there. I want to give them input that will pull it out. I want them to discover the leader inside of them as early as possible.

Reflect and Respond

1. Think of one idea you could use to create a memory for your child.

2. What is one way you could capitalize on teachable moments?

3. How can you help your kids consume material that will help them grow as leaders?

12

BUILDING YOUR INVESTMENT PLAN

*Could I climb to the highest place in Athens, I would lift my
voice and proclaim: "Fellow citizens, why do you turn to scrape
every stone to gather wealth, and take so little care of your children,
to whom one day you must relinquish it all?"*

—SOCRATES

A NEW KIND OF CHILD HAS BEEN BORN OVER the last twenty years. I've referred to them as the millennial generation. However, these kids are being molded by more than mere sociological factors. It's not just the culture that's shaping them. "Parents have, to a large extent, lost confidence in themselves and in their good judgment," says Peter Gorski, a committee chair of the American Academy of Pediatrics. There is a phenomenon occurring in the American home today that's producing a driven child.

These kids drew media attention in 1994, when the Carnegie Corporation published a report describing a "quiet crisis" among U.S. children. The study concluded that children were being ill-served by two-income parents who were so busy raising revenue that they neglected to raise kids. The press ran alarming stories about young children being left at home alone. Do you remember those days? The White House called a conference on childhood development. In response, parents started buying all kinds of educational devices, from books to classical music CDs, to make sure their kid was OK. They felt they could make up for their inadequacies by purchasing educational toys. The thought was: If I don't have the latest Mozart CD, my child may go to jail rather than Yale!

By 1998, Julie Aigner-Clark sold one million dollars' worth of her Baby Mozart and Baby Einstein videos. Georgia governor Zell Miller allocated $105,000 in his new budget proposal to give every newborn a classical CD or cassette. During the next year, the "Mozart Effect" report was published, saying test scores would improve if kids could make music rather than just listen to it. Consequently, toy companies began cranking out instruments for toddlers. Parents bought them. Everyone wanted their kid to have all the advantages they could give.

Recently, parents have discovered what all this did to their kids, as they became young adults. Alexandria Robbins and Abby Winter wrote about it in *Quarterlife Crisis: The Unique Challenges of Life in Your Twenties*. It outlines how dissatisfied eighteen- to thirty-year-olds are with their life and their performance on the job. The pressure to excel has produced a first wave of young adults who are just short of clinically depressed.[1]

Recently, *Time* magazine carried a cover article, "So You Want to Raise a Super Kid"[2] in which Jeffrey Kluger and Alice Park amended some of this parenting hype. They wrote that child-development experts considered those sterile tools inferior to more social and emotional activities such as talking with or reading to children. In other words, nothing takes the place of old-fashioned relationship and time. The only thing shown to optimize children's intellectual potential is a secure, trusting relationship with their parents.

Asked in a recent study what skills children need in order to be prepared for school, parents of kindergartners routinely cited achievements such as knowing numbers, letters, colors, and shapes. Teachers, however, disagree. Far more important, they say, are social skills, such as sharing, interacting with others, and following instructions. "Intelligence is based on emotional adequacy," says child development expert T. Berry Brazelton. "The concept of emotional intelligence is at the base of all of this."[3]

I share this with you to encourage you. Far more important for children than academic ability are skills children learn from their *parents and family units.* I believe no matter what new toy or computer gadget our technological world can create—the greatest gift you can give your child as they mature into leaders is intentional time and relationship. Learning best occurs when a parent has a plan to personally invest in their child.

I want to create environments conducive to growing strong kids out of Bethany and Jonathan, and I want to respond to the critical periods in their life when a particular kind of guidance is needed. I try to make my plan appropriate for my kids' maturity level, since they develop differently at different ages:

1. The Age of Regulation—ages 1 to 7

2. The Age of Imitation—ages 8 to 12

3. The Age of Inspiration—ages 13 and up

I have a question for you. What's your plan? Now that we have covered what you need to know, what your child needs to know, and when to pass on the principles, you must develop a plan to pass the principles on. The good news is, I intend to help you with your plan in this chapter. I'll enable you to structure a mentoring plan that includes the key principles and key times to share them for the appropriate stage your kids are in.

FAMILIES THAT BUILD LEADERS

Fifteen years ago, Nick Stinnett and John Defrain did some research among families. At the time, Nick was professor of Human Development and Family Life at the University of Alabama. John was associate professor in the Department of Human Development and the Family at the University of Nebraska. They placed a brief notice in four dozen newspapers in twenty-five states. They requested the following: If you live in a strong family, please contact us. We know a lot about what makes families fail. We need to know more about what makes them succeed. Letters poured in. A questionnaire was mailed to each family who responded, and the Family Strengths Research project was born. More than three thousand families participated.

One of the most surprising things to emerge was that six key qualities for making a strong family environment were mentioned time and time again. Where they existed, the families functioned well and passed on their strengths to their children. I will use the six qualities as my framework here. Let's build our plan around them.

Six Qualities That Build Strong Children

1. Commitment.

If we hope to nurture leaders in our homes, we must begin with commitment. Strong families are committed to each other. They possess identity and unity. They have a sense of being a team. Children see their parents as leaders who coach family members into cooperation. Think about it. The first place your kids are going to see leadership is in your home!

Let's talk about your plan to build this into your time with your child. If they are going to learn how to lead, they must learn commitment. When they are young, they can show relative commitment, based on their age. A five-year-old can't keep long commitments, but they can learn to follow through on commitments to feed a goldfish, straighten their room, take a bath, and brush their teeth. By middle-school years, commitments are tougher, such as caring for a small pet, completing a list of chores, or even baby-sitting younger children. By the teen years, longer-term commitments such as semester- and year-long commitments should be doable. We increase their chances to do so, however, when we parents model commitment first.

A sixth-grade teacher I know, in an upper-middle-class California city, asked her class to complete a creative writing assignment by finishing the sentence: "I wish . . . " The teacher expected the kids to respond with wishes for bicycles, dogs, television sets, and trips to Hawaii. She couldn't have been more wrong. A full twenty out of thirty children made references to their own disintegrating families. Some samples were:

- "I wish my family wouldn't fight, and I wish my dad would come back."

- "I wish my mother wouldn't switch boyfriends."

- "I wish I could get straight A's, so my father would love me."

- "I wish I had one mom and one dad so the kids wouldn't make fun of me."

- "I have three moms and three dads and they botch up my life."

If we fail to model commitment as parents, we cannot assume our children will get it from us. When Mother Teresa received her Nobel Peace Prize in 1979, she was asked: "What can we do to promote world peace?" Her answer? "Go home and love your family."

Your Investment Plan

1. When do I model this for my family? When can I better demonstrate it for them?

2. How can I best draw commitment from my child at this stage of their life?

2. Appreciation.

A second characteristic of strong families is expressed appreciation for one another. Our game plan must include creating an environment where you can share what you have noticed about the qualities and progress in your kids. Everyone works better in an environment of praise and encouragement. Encouragement is the oxygen of the soul. It fans into flame the strengths of those who receive it. Unfortunately, this is often the first thing to go in the American household. We fail to notice what becomes too familiar. Someone once said, "Home is a place where family members go when they are tired of being nice to other people." How sad but true. Family should be the place where we constantly practice the art of appreciation and encouragement—for they are the ones we live with and to whom we will give our inheritance! We seem to run out of manners with those in our own homes. Do we get tired of them? Yes. Are we transparent about it? Yes. Can we get nasty? No.

When we express appreciation, we produce a secure atmosphere. Emotional security is an early trait of a healthy leader. Our appreciation should be sincere, specific, public, and personal. Here are the kinds of things I try to express appreciation for, in my kids:

1. Their inward strengths

2. Their outward skills

3. Their unique achievements

4. Their personal style

Our children may not say much at the time, but down inside, they soak up our words of appreciation. They also soak up the quiet ways we communicate their value, and provide a model for them, as emerging young leaders. One young author tried to put it this way:

When you thought I wasn't looking, I saw you hang my painting on the refrigerator,
And I wanted to paint another one.

When you thought I wasn't looking, I saw you make my favorite cake,
And I knew I was special because you took care of all the details.

When you thought I wasn't looking, I heard you say a prayer,
And I believed there was a God I could always talk to.

When you thought I wasn't looking, I felt you kiss me goodnight,
And I felt loved.

When you thought I wasn't looking, I saw tears come from your eyes,
And I learned that sometimes things hurt, but it is all right to cry.

When you thought I wasn't looking, I noticed you cared,
And I wanted to be everything I could be.

When you thought I wasn't looking, I looked . . .
And wanted to say thanks for all the things I saw when you thought I
wasn't looking.[4]

Your Investment Plan

1. When do I express appreciation for my child's strengths?

2. How can I plan to spot and express my affirmation to them?

3. Time Together.

A survey was taken of fifteen hundred children. They were asked:
What makes a happy family? None of them replied, "Money, lots of toys,
computer games, big houses, or cars." Instead, the vast majority said:
"Doing things together."

It is so simple, we miss it. Far too often, I try to do the sensational when
my family prefers the sentimental. I'm in a hurry and miss what they really
want. I can identify with the person who defined the American home as:
"A domestic cloverleaf on which we pass one another, en route to meetings." Ouch. I remember when my daughter, Bethany, was four years old.
She and her mother took me to the airport for another trip. It was the
fourth time they had done it that month. As we sat in the coffee shop
inside the airport, Bethany looked around and asked me: "Dad, do you
live here?"

When we spend time with our kids, we speak volumes about their
importance. We lift their esteem and confidence. They get the chance to
gain a stronger sense of identity. All leaders need to obtain this sooner or
later. I believe it is best received in the home. Gary Smalley and John
Trent wrote *The Blessing*, in which they describe the Jewish custom fathers
used to practice with their sons.[5] They would speak words of blessing to
them, as young men, that would often shape their future. Jacob lined up
his twelve sons and blessed each one of them. They later became the

fathers of the twelve tribes of Israel! Smalley and Trent indicate the five components of the blessing:

1. Affirming Words—Dad would affirm their strengths.

2. Meaningful Touch—Dad would embrace and kiss them.

3. Expression of High Value—Dad would state the value each child added.

4. Picture of a Special Future—Dad would share the potential he saw in them.

5. Genuine Commitment—Dad would stay committed to see them mature.

As your child matures, you'll find they will reach seasons where they need your time even more than others. For instance, each time they reach a junction in their education, they often need special time. At the start of kindergarten, middle school, and high school, it is good to invest extra time with them. If you stay sensitive, you will spot when they need extra time from you. That's when you need to push "pause" on your agenda if possible, and give it to them. You may never get that moment back.

Your Investment Plan

1. How am I using the four junctions (Chapter Ten) of time in my daily routine?

2. Do I regularly spend quality time, sharing with my child? When?

4. Communication.

Do you model good communication to your kids? Do you not only talk to them, but do you provide an example of communication as you interact with your spouse? The average couple married ten years or more spends only thirty-seven minutes a week in close communication. One husband confessed, "My wife says I don't listen to her. At least, I think that's what she said."

As we nurture our kids in leadership, communication is an essential ingredient. Good leaders communicate. We must make our homes safe places where communication takes place regularly. This is where we must determine four things:

- Where will we communicate? (Do you have a safe place to talk?)
- When will we communicate? (How about the four junctions in Chapter Ten?)
- How will we communicate? (Do you have effective, creative methods?)
- What will we communicate? (What are the life principles they need?)

Sometimes, we do this by accident. When we don't plan to communicate specific principles, we end up communicating something we don't wish to pass on. For instance, one writer humorously remembers how his mom taught him about life:

My mother taught me about receiving: *You're going to get it when we get home!*

My mother taught me about logic: *If you fall off that swing and break your neck, you're not going to the store with me!*

My mother taught me about medical science: *If you don't stop crossing your eyes, they are going to freeze that way!*

My mother taught me how to think ahead: *If you don't pass your spelling test, you'll never get a good job.*

My mother taught me about my roots: *Do you think you were born in a barn?*

My mother taught me how to become an adult: *If you don't eat your vegetables, you'll never grow up!*

My mother taught me about genetics: *You're just like your father!*

And my all-time favorite, justice: *One day you'll have kids, and I hope they turn out just like you! Then, you'll see what it's like!*

I suggest you take a few minutes and write out some of the most crucial principles you want to pass on to your child. You may want to review

Chapters Five through Seven for ideas. Ask yourself: What will build their character? What will enable them to influence their world? I picked up a great book by Jay McGraw last year. He is the son of author Phillip McGraw, who wrote the book, *Life Strategies*. Jay's book is written to teens, and is called *Life Strategies for Teens*. In it, he suggests ten life laws:

1. You either get it or you don't. (Be real and figure out what makes you tick.)

2. You create your own experience. (Don't be a victim—reach for what you want.)

3. People do what works. (You are only addicted if you don't take responsibility.)

4. You cannot change what you do not acknowledge. (Be honest about your faults.)

5. Life rewards action. (You can't earn a thing by sitting around. Get up and work.)

6. There is no reality, only perception. (Our perception determines our outcome.)

7. Life is managed, not cured. (Life isn't easy. Keep it in gear—no coasting.)

8. We teach people how to treat us. (Others believe about you what you do.)

9. There is power in forgiveness. (We must let go of past hurt and offenses.)

10. You have to name it before you can claim it. (Figure out what you really want.)[6]

Your Investment Plan

1. What are my kids ready to learn? What am I ready to communicate?

2. How can I use the four junctions to share it?

5. Coping Skills.

Families that are strong master this one. They build into their kids the ability to see something positive in crises, to pull together, to remain flexible, to draw on spiritual and communication strengths, and to get help from friends and professionals. They do what it takes to make it together. By the way—this is exactly the kind of quality we should nurture in our kids. Every family has problems. Healthy families endure them. Strong families not only endure them but use them as a teaching tool for their kids.

As children mature into leaders, problem solving is one of the most crucial skills they can learn. Problem solving must be modeled. I believe it is healthy for them to see conflict dealt with in an open and constructive way. Don't sweep it under the rug and pretend it isn't there. This will not help them cope with the world. Don't destroy each other through it. This will make them afraid to address it. Help them to learn how to hang in there and resolve it.

Author Dr. John C. Maxwell shared with me a story from his childhood. He and his older brother Larry would wrestle in the living room every week. Because he was younger and smaller, John would lose every time. After several months of this, his father could see he was losing his passion to win. Because he had no expectation of ever winning, he would give up from the beginning and get pinned. Finally, one night his dad did something wise. He asked Larry to step aside. He wanted to see if he could whip John, too. The older brother eagerly waited to see his dad wrestle his little brother down and pin him.

Interestingly, it was a close fight—until finally John got the best of his dad and pinned him on the ground. Grinning from ear to ear, John got up having finally tasted victory. He marveled at how a little kid like him could actually beat his dad! Obviously, his father knew exactly what he was doing. He had created a close fight but allowed John to struggle and win. Afterward, John remembers that Larry never pinned his younger brother again.

When we demonstrate coping skills, we transfer four qualities to our kids:

1. The willingness to endure

2. The ability to negotiate

3. The capacity to strategize

4. The passion to resolve conflict

Your Investment Plan

1. When will I develop coping skills in my kids?

2. How have I demonstrated this skill? How will I model this?

6. Spiritual Health.

A final ingredient of strong families is spiritual vitality. I believe this, too, is essential for a young leader to be complete. The spiritual climate in your home will set the tone for your child to develop a good heart. Learning to trust God will build their faith, foster a love for others, deepen their humility, and establish a vision for the future.

When your children see you pray, they see you model another vital behavior. They see their "authority" demonstrating submission to an even higher authority and setting an example for them when they are called to submit. My kids have walked in on me several times as I study Scripture in my office at home. It gives us a chance to pray together and maybe even talk about what I am reading. We are all students. Often, we will spontaneously play a little game called "spin the globe." I have a globe that they'll spin around several times. Next, they will point to one spot with their index finger until the globe finally stops rotating. I have to tell them whatever I know about the needs of the country they are pointing to when it stops, and then we pray for that country.

One of the reasons I want my kids to develop an authentic relationship with God is because one day I will not be with them. They'll grow older and leave home. One day, I will die. I want them to continue a vital relationship with their heavenly Father, who will always be with them. I want them to recognize there is a transcendent set of values that doesn't change with the times, and by which they can evaluate their character. I believe this will only enhance their leadership. This will furnish perspective on why they ought to influence their world. It will enlarge their soul and help them live for causes bigger than themselves.

Your Investment Plan

1. What kind of spiritual depth do I model for my children?

2. Does God have the final authority in our home?

HOME SECURITY

These six qualities make for a very "SECURE" culture in the home. They breed a fertile ground for raising up healthy young leaders. I have found the little acronym for "SECURE" to be very helpful as I parent my kids:

S—Spend time together

E—Express positive thoughts

C—Consistently discipline

U—Unite during a crisis

R—Recognize each person's value

E—Encourage them daily

If we will do this, we'll leave the legacy we desire in our kids. In his book, *Who Switched the Price Tags*, Anthony Campolo related the words of a black Baptist preacher speaking to his congregation. "Children," he said, "you're going to die! . . . One of these days, they're going to take you down to the cemetery, drop you in a hole, throw some dirt on your face, and go back to the church and eat potato salad.

"When you were born," he continued, "you alone were crying and everybody else was happy. The important question I want to ask you is this: when you die, are you alone going to be happy, leaving everyone else crying? The answer depends on whether you live to gain titles or testimonies. When they lay you in the grave, are people going to stand around giving testimonies of the good things you did for them? . . . Will you leave behind just a newspaper column telling people how important you were, or will you leave crying people who give testimonies of how they've lost the best friend they ever had?"

There's nothing wrong with titles. Titles are good things to have. But if it ever comes down to a choice between a title and a testimony—go for the testimony.

Reflect and Respond

1. What kind of environment have you created in your home? Is it secure? Is it stressful? Is it safe to talk?

2. Which of the six characteristics of a strong home do you practice effectively? Which of them do you need to improve?

3. What is the next step in your plan to invest in your children?

PART 4

HOW TO PASS IT ON

13

SIX GIFTS YOU CAN GIVE THEM

A mentor is a brain to pick, a shoulder to cry on,
and a kick in the seat of the pants.
—JOHN CROSBY

I SAW A MOVIE IN 1996 THAT INSPIRED me deeply. Maybe you saw it, too. It was called *Mr. Holland's Opus*. Richard Dreyfuss plays a musician who wants to move to New York and become a composer. He is honest about his quest to compose a famous symphony and get rich. He winds up becoming a high-school music teacher to save some money until he and his wife can move away and fulfill his dreams.

Somewhere en route, his values change. He begins to see the needs of his students and feels compelled to help them. Almost against his will, he becomes a mentor for many of them. He invests extra time after class, giving them personal time and direction. He persists in his belief in them until many of them become "somebody" following their graduation. As it turns out, he never leaves for New York. He continues teaching for thirty years.

Toward the end of the film, Mr. Holland is forced to resign due to cutbacks in the school budget. He is devastated. He moans to a colleague, "You know, it's funny. They drug me into this thing kicking and screaming—and now it's the only thing I want to do." He paused and said, "Just the minute you think that what you do really counts, you get a wake-up call. You suddenly realize you're mistaken. You are expendable." He feels he's wasted his life in this small town, working with ungrateful teenagers. Maybe he should have gone to New York after all. At least he would have some money now.

He gathers his belongings and walks out of the school for the last time when he hears music coming from the auditorium. At that moment, the story climaxes. He opens the door and is shocked. The room is full of hundreds and hundreds of students and alumni who have returned to say "thanks" for his investment in them. They applaud as he walks in to this surprise farewell event. The state governor, his former student, steps up to the podium to speak: "I've heard rumors that Mr. Holland somehow feels his life is misspent; even a failure, because he always wanted to go to New York and get rich and famous composing a symphony. As you know, Mr. Holland never got to New York; he never got rich off of his salary here; and he never got famous outside of this school." Then, she paused and looked right at her former teacher. "But, Mr. Holland. If you feel you're a failure, that is where you are wrong." In tears, she paused again. "Just look around you. We are your symphony. We are your opus."

Mr. Holland is struck with the overwhelming results of his decision to stay and invest in the lives of kids. He chose them over money and fame. The deposits he made over time had now paid great dividends. He had made the right decision.

I love this movie, because it's the story of a reluctant mentor. He was hesitant and awkward at first. Like you and me, this teacher didn't feel he knew what he was doing as he worked with those teenagers. Yet, somehow, he had left a legacy by pouring "life lessons" into those kids. Every time I watch this movie on video, I think about my impact on my own kids and the students I teach each week. I want so much to leave a memorable impression on them, and I'm always looking for ways to do that. I know this means that I must actively pursue the role of a mentor in their lives. Parenting is ultimate mentoring.

SIX GIFTS YOU CAN GIVE AWAY

Because I believe young leaders are raised up one life at a time, through life-on-life mentoring, I have made it my aim to distill what makes for a good mentoring experience. As I spend time with my kids, I have boiled it down to half a dozen "gifts" I try to give them. I believe if we'll give these gifts away, we will participate in changing their lives forever . . . and build a leader in the process!

1. Paint Pictures.

The human mind thinks in pictures most of the time. If I say the word "elephant" to my kids, they don't picture the letters e-l-e-p-h-a-n-t. Instead, they picture a big, gray animal. Why? We are visual people living in a visual age. By the time we reach adulthood, we are able to think more abstractly, but even adults enjoy and remember stories, analogies, and metaphors. They help us retain important information. As I mentioned before, the younger children are, the more they need a picture to grasp a concept. Our minds don't think in concepts until we are well into adolescence. So, I've decided to become an artist and paint pictures that last.

I do this most often by telling stories. Very often, when my kids need to learn a new concept, I will teach it with a story. (In Chapter Eleven, I covered what kinds of stories are most effective with kids.) If I can, I'll tell a story they can identify with from my own childhood. For instance, both of my kids have taken a few risky steps in their lives already. Fear of the unknown caused them to withdraw and consider quitting, or avoid signing up for a baseball team, or dismissing a huge science project, or dodging a friend to resolve a conflict, or not taking a part in a stage play.

This happened just two weeks ago, as my son tried out for a music team that would perform and do choreography on stage. We sat down, and I told him about my first audition, when I was in the fourth grade. It was a play at my school, and I had to try out in front of seventy-five other hopeful candidates. The director was a stern man who had little patience. I was so flustered that I went blank on the words. In a split second, I decided to make up my own. I sang with authority and passion—it was all I had at the moment, with a brain on the blink! I made the play, because the director saw I could improvise with confidence! My son and I laughed at my predicament, and he grew calm about his own audition. He did well, and he made the team.

John F. Kennedy spoke about growing up with his grandfather. His granddad introduced a little game to him called "throw your cap over the wall." He said it was a game to spark courage. As young kids, the Kennedys would pass by many large homes on their walk to school. Several times, one of them began to wonder out loud about what was behind the huge fences surrounding the houses. Finally, one of the boys grabbed Kennedy's hat and threw it over the wall. He said, "You gotta fetch your cap. Now you'll get to go find out what's behind that wall!" In that frightening moment, the young boy would climb the wall, grab his cap, and look around for a minute. He had beaten his fear because he had to.

> *Identify a way you can provide a picture of leadership for your kids.*

JFK said this little game provided a picture for him as a leader. There were many times he would have to take a step that would force him to display courage and follow through on his commitments. He called that step "throwing his cap over the wall." It was a lasting picture.

2. Provide Handles.

Children need handles in order to grab hold of leadership truths. Simply put, "handles" are things we can grab on to, and make something happen. Every drawer or door has a handle. When you grab one, you can cause movement. We give our kids "handles" when we summarize a complex principle into a user-friendly fashion. Every child possesses some knowledge of truth. Most of them, however, are hard pressed to put it into words, in such a way as to use it in everyday life. FamilyWise, a nonprofit organization, does this with thirty-six core values they teach kids, ages five to twelve. Each value has an easy-to-remember definition. For instance, discipline means: "doing what you know you should, even when you don't feel like it." Kids learn the definition, watch videos, sketches, and sing songs about it. Singing about a principle is one of the best ways to provide handles on a truth. Kids memorize information so quickly when they can sing about it. At home, I make up jingles that my kids sing. We laugh and learn at the same time. The more hilarious the rhyme, the more memorable the principle! (You can check out FamilyWise on their Web page: www.familywise.org.)

Another way to provide a handle for your kids is to do something with them that is memorable and transferable. The experience becomes a handle to use and pass on to others. One father searched for a way to teach his son to control his temper.

The boy's anger was like a time bomb that could blow up at any moment. His dad knew this would sabotage his life, his leadership, and his career as an adult. So, at age ten, the father gave his son a bag of nails and told him that every time he lost his temper to hammer a nail into the fence in their backyard. The first week, the boy had driven thirty-seven nails into the fence. Then, it gradually dwindled down. He discovered it was easier to hold his temper than to drive those nails into the fence. Finally, the day came when the boy didn't lose his temper at all. He spoke to his father about it, and his dad suggested his son now pull out one nail for each day that he was able to control his temper. The days passed, and the ten-year-old was finally able to tell his father all the nails were gone.

The father took his son by the hand and led him to the fence. "You've really done well, son. I'm proud of you for getting hold of your anger. But I want you to notice something. Look at the holes in the fence. The fence will never be the same. When you say things in anger, they leave a scar just like these. When someone stabs a man in the back, he can draw out the knife, but no matter how many times he says he's sorry, a wound is still there." That day, the young son got a "handle" on his temper: A verbal wound is as bad as a physical one.

> *Name two handles you can give your child to help explain leadership principles.*

3. Supply Road Maps.

Road maps give us direction on our journey. Road maps actually fill four functions on a trip. They help you identify where you are and clearly assess your location. They give you a big-picture view of the entire journey. You can see an entire state in one piece of paper. They show you what roads you might take to get to your desired destination. Incidentally, notice I said "roads" plural, not singular. There are often several roads you can take to get to a goal. We must not make those decisions for our children. And they illustrate which roads to avoid if you want to get to a certain destination. Some roads just won't take you there.

Do you see my analogy? This is precisely the role we must play in our children's lives. Since we've traveled down many roads before them, we can give them vision for the good roads and bad roads along the way. I saw this vividly illustrated just before the 1988 Winter Olympics; a TV program featured blind skiers being trained for slalom skiing, impossible as that sounds. Paired with sighted skiers, the blind skiers were taught on the flats how to make right and left turns. When that feat was mastered, they were taken to the slalom slope, where their sighted partners skied beside them shouting "Left!" and "Right!" As they followed the directions, they were able to negotiate the course and cross the finish line, depending solely on the sighted skier's word! It was either trust or tragedy.

What a vivid picture of the trust we must build with our kids, if we're to supply road maps they will use. This is so difficult that many parents simply give up by the time their kids become teenagers. The trust and relationship both diminish. Unfortunately, just the time the child most needs some navigation—they get nothing. The Minnesota Crime Commission, presumably neutral on any spiritual or moral issue, stated the following to explain heightened crime statistics: "Every baby starts life as a little savage. He is completely selfish and self-centered. He wants what he wants when he wants it—his bottle, his mother's affection, a playmate's toy, his uncle's watch. Deny these, and he seethes with rage and aggressiveness, which would be murderous were he not so helpless. He is, in fact, dirty. He has no morals, no knowledge, no skills. This means that all children, not just certain children, are born delinquent. If permitted to continue in the self-centered world of his infancy, given free rein to his impulsive actions, to satisfy his wants, every child would grow up a criminal, a thief, a killer, a rapist."[1]

> *What's one road map you need to give to your son or daughter?*

This may sound harsh, but when I paused to think about it, the statistics bear out the truth of these conclusions. The day after the Columbine High School tragedy, when I heard how teen killers Eric Harris and Dylan Klebold created bombs in their garages and basements—I didn't want to punish the teens as much as I wanted to punish their parents! How could they be so out of touch? I wondered. Parents must become mentors who supply road maps in life.

Bill Gates, in his book, *Business @ the Speed of Thought,* lays out eleven rules that students do not learn in high school. He argues that our feel-good, politically correct teachings have created a generation of kids with little concept of reality, and they are set up for failure without a road map. I had to laugh at these tongue-in-cheek rules, but I quickly passed them on to my kids:

1. Life is not fair. Get used to it.

2. The world won't care about your self-esteem. The world will expect you to accomplish something *before* you feel good about yourself.

3. You will not make $40,000 a year right out of high school. You won't be vice president with a car phone, until you earn both.

4. If you think your teacher is tough, wait till you get a boss. He doesn't have tenure.

5. Flipping burgers is not beneath your dignity. Your grandparents had a different word for burger flipping: they called it opportunity.

6. If you mess up, it's not your parents' fault, so don't whine about your mistakes, learn from them.

7. Before you were born, your parents weren't as boring as they are now. They got that way from paying your bills, cleaning your clothes, and listening to you talk about how cool you are. So before you save the rain forest from the parasites of your parents' generation—try "delousing" the closet in your own room.

8. Your school may have done away with winners and losers, but life has not. In some schools they have abolished failing grades; they'll give you as many times as you want to get the right answer. This doesn't bear the slightest resemblance to *anything* in real life.

9. Life is not divided into semesters. You don't get summers off and very few employers are interested in helping you find yourself. Do that on your own time.

10. Television is *not* real life. In real life people actually have to leave the coffee shop and go to jobs.

11. Be nice to nerds. Chances are you'll end up working for one.

4. Furnish Laboratories.

Another gift I try to give my kids is a laboratory. We furnish "laboratories" for our children when we give them a place to practice the principles we've discussed with them. Do you remember science class in college? I do. Both a lecture and a laboratory were mandatory. The lecture was the boring part. All we did was listen to the professor talk from a textbook. The "lab" was the fun part. We got to *do* what was in the textbook! We got to use Bunsen burners, chemicals, and test tubes . . . and blow a few things up! I define them this way: laboratories are safe places in which to experiment. Unfortunately, our world (whether it is school, home, or church) offers many "lectures" but very few "labs." In these labs, we learn the right questions to ask, the appropriate ways to do things, an understanding of the real world, how life works, and even how to fail. This might be as simple as role playing a particular situation or feeding the homeless in a soup kitchen. Each time I mentor students, I plan ideas for laboratories that correspond with the principles we discuss. This forces me to be creative, but it's worth it. I believe they need a safe place to try out the principle!

A friend of mine once had a conversation with a trapeze artist from the circus. The performer admitted the net underneath was there to keep them from breaking their necks but said: "The net also keeps us from falling. It gives us confidence. Imagine there is no net. We would be so nervous that we would be more likely to miss and fall. If there wasn't a net, we would not dare to do some of the things we do. But because there's a net—we dare to make two turns, and once I made three turns—thanks to the net!"

Simply put, the net furnishes the security needed to experiment. It's a safe place, every time. Let's face it. Our kids will soon enough enter a world that is unsafe, where one wrong move can ruin them. Let's give them a chance to take a risk and experiment when the cost is low. A safe leadership laboratory could be as simple as letting them choose sides for a baseball game; allowing them to plan the summer vacation; turning them loose with a budget for a school project; or helping them start a neighborhood soccer team.

There's another reason why kids need laboratories. They generally don't learn until they do something. Mere cerebral stimulation frequently doesn't really change people. We must do more than just engage their heads, but their wills and their hearts as well. I believe in the axiom: information without application leads to constipation! Put another way, if we eat, we need to exercise as well. Case in point: In 1987, a Soviet cosmonaut returned to earth after 326 days in orbit. He was in good health thanks to a new "penguin suit" designed to help them run and exercise while in space. Five years earlier, two cosmonauts suffered from dizziness, high pulse rates, and heart palpitations when they returned home after only 211 days. They couldn't walk for a week! Why? Their muscles had atrophied, and their heart had weakened from zero exercise. When there is no gravity, the muscles of the body begin to waste away because there is no resistance, no push, no exercise. So it is with life.

> *Name one laboratory you can create to help your child experiment in leadership.*

5. Give Roots.

Roots are crucial to nearly anything that grows. As we mentor our children, we often hear the term "roots and wings" placed side by side. This popular phrase describes everyone's need for foundations to be laid, and for the freedom to soar and broaden their horizons. Roots are the foundation. They represent the heritage and basic worldview that helps them construct a character-based life, rather than an emotion-based life. They are the firm ground on which your children can stand. Roots provide strength. We give roots when we help our kids possess strong convictions by which they can live their lives, and the self-esteem to stand behind those convictions, even when others don't. Someone once said: Parents need to fill a child's bucket of self-esteem so high that the rest of the world can't poke holes in it to drain it dry. While Bill Gates may be right—the world won't care about their self-esteem—I believe parents must build it into their kids so they are secure enough to take a risk in the world.

The roots my wife and I are building into our kids revolve around our family core values, such as honesty, positive attitude, service, responsibility, gratitude, and obedience. For us, each of these stems from a deep relationship with God. When these roots grow deep, they provide the strength our kids will need when the winds of adversity blow. The deeper the roots, the taller the tree can grow and the more durable that tree is in a storm.

George Jaeger discovered this on a night he would describe as his worst nightmare. It was late afternoon when his boat's engine sputtered, stalled, and refused to restart. A storm had beaten the boat. Gallons of water surged into the craft, as it pitched on huge waves. The five Jaegers had done all they knew to do, but it wasn't enough. An exciting fishing trip was now a thing of horror. They were going under.

Grim-faced, George Jaeger, his three sons, and his elderly father methodically tightened the buckles on their life jackets, tied themselves together with a rope, and slipped into a black and boiling Atlantic. Very little was said. It grew dark. First, one boy and then another swallowed too much salt water, gagged, and strangled on the brine as they fought to keep their heads up. The helpless father heard his sons, one by one, then his dad choke and drown. But George couldn't surrender. After eight nightmarish hours, he staggered onto the shore, still pulling the rope that bound him to the bodies of the other four.

"I realized they were all dead—my three boys and my father—but I guess I didn't want to accept it, so I kept on swimming all night long," he later told reporters. "My youngest boy, Clifford, was the first to go. I had always taught our children not to fear death because it meant being with the Lord." Before young Cliff died, his dad heard him say, "I'd rather be with Jesus than go on fighting."

In that vivid Atlantic memory, George Jaeger had a chance to witness the impact of his fifteen years as a father. The boys died quietly, with courage and dignity. Up to the last minute, one by one they modeled the truth passed on by their father: when under pressure stay calm, think . . . even if death is near, keep under control. So they did, and so they died. When the ultimate test was administered in an angry sea, they handed in perfect scores.

In her best-selling book, *What Is a Family?*, Edith Schaeffer shares the idea that a family is a "perpetual relay of truth." A place where principles are hammered and honed on the anvil of everyday living. Where character traits are sculptured under the watchful eyes of moms and dads. Where steel-strong fibers are woven into the fabric of inner constitution. This is the stuff leaders are made of. Are you building these roots into your child?

6. Offer Wings.

We give our kids wings when we enable them to think big, attempt big things, and expect big things from God and themselves. When someone possesses wings, they're free to explore and to plumb the depths of their own potential, without fear of failure. When parents give wings, they help their child soar to new heights in their life. They applaud as their children pass them by and exceed what they have accomplished.

Some of America's most notable leaders have said they owe their success to their parents. Presidents whose leadership has changed the course of our history were "mama's boys" by their own confession, and pushed forward due to the confidence, the resources, the correction, and the mentoring from mom. James Garfield said he made it because of his mother's "blind confidence" in him. Even on his deathbed, his agony could only be overcome by writing to his mother. Teddy Roosevelt felt he was a carbon copy of his mother. William Howard Taft's mother said he needed "constant watching and correcting . . . but we can't love our children too much." Woodrow Wilson drew upon his mother's strength into adulthood. He said he came to appreciate the strength of womanhood through his mother's apron strings. Franklin D. Roosevelt wouldn't even dare go to school without his mother . . . and the school was Harvard University! She went with him, organizing his life, as he attended college! While he was an extreme case, he again illustrates the drive and the wings a man can receive from a parent. She almost pushed him into greatness. Similar things could be said about Harry Truman, Dwight Eisenhower, John F. Kennedy, and Lyndon Johnson. I believe something great lies in every child, but those that make it often owe the victory to their mother's extra nudge and to the roots she establishes in their life.

I mentioned earlier that each night, after I've tucked my kids into bed, I pray: "Lord, give my children more influence than their mother and father combined." This may sound silly. I don't know what their calling in life is yet, but I do know I want them to play an influential role in their world. I want them to soar above where I have gone. I want to take the lid off of their thinking and let them dream and attempt what they might not attempt without a little encouragement. This means, however, that I must let go one day and allow them to venture out on their own, as adults. They will have their own dreams, their own abilities, their own style. My job is not control, but empowerment!

David Thomas, in *Marriage and Family Living*, writes:

> Recently, our daughter received a document of almost infinite worth to a typical fifteen-year-old: a learner's permit for driving. Shortly thereafter, I accompanied her as she drove for the first time.
>
> In the passenger seat, having no steering wheel and no brakes, I was in her hands—a strange feeling for a parent, both disturbing and surprisingly satisfying. As she looked to see if the road was clear, we slowly pulled away from the curb. Meanwhile, I checked to see if the sky was falling or the earth quaking. If getting from here to there was the only thing that mattered, I would gladly have taken the wheel. But there were other matters of importance here, most of them having to do with my own paternal "letting go."
>
> I experienced a strange combination of weakness and power. My understanding of weakness was simple: she was in control, I was not. But she was able to move to this level of adulthood because of what my wife and I had done. Our power had empowered her. Her newfound strength was attained from us. So as we pulled away from the curb, we all gained in stature.[2]

Professor Howard Hendricks, of Dallas Theological Seminary, remembers getting a package from home, when he first arrived at college. When he opened it, he realized it was a package from his mother. In it were two apron strings. She was simply saying: Son, I am cutting the apron strings. I love you, but I am letting you go to soar and become the man you have the potential to become.

GIVING AND RECEIVING

These are gifts you can give to your child. They require you to step into the role of a mentor. How well the gifts are received depends on the relationship and influence you have with your child. Pictures, handles, road maps, laboratories, roots, and wings are just nice word pictures unless they are received by those young hearts we attempt to shape. In the next chapter, we'll consider what we can do to deepen our influence in their lives.

Reflect and Respond

1. Which of these word pictures do you do naturally?

2. Can you think of one way you can practice each one of them with your child?

3. What is most difficult about mentoring your child? What prevents you from doing it well?

14

DEEPENING YOUR INFLUENCE
IN THEIR LIVES

The parent who pushes to exert his power
most drastically over children loses all power over them,
except the power to twist, and hurt and destroy.
—GARRY WILLS

SOONER OR LATER, EVERY ONE OF US LONGS to have a deeper influence in the life of someone else. For parents, it often happens as their sons and daughters become teens. Their voices fade as new voices clamor for their attention. Sometimes, it happens earlier if we don't know how to connect with our children. We may know what needs to be said, but not how to say it.

In the movie *City Slickers*, comedian Billy Crystal played the part of a bored baby boomer who sells radio advertising time. On the day he visits his son's school to talk about his work along with other fathers, he suddenly lets loose a deadpan monologue to the bewildered youngsters in the class:

Value this time in your life, kids, because this is the time in your life when you still have choices. It goes by so fast. When you're a teenager, you think you can do anything and you do. Your twenties are a blur. Thirties, you raise your family, you make a little money, and you think to yourself, "What happened to my twenties?" Forties, you grow a little pot belly, you grow another chin. The music starts to get too loud, and one of your old girlfriends from high school becomes a grandmother. Fifties, you have minor surgery—you call it a procedure, but it's surgery. Sixties, you'll have major surgery, the music is still loud, but it doesn't matter because you can't hear it anyway. Seventies, you and the wife retire to Ft. Lauderdale. You start eating dinner at 2:00 in the afternoon, you have lunch around 10:00, breakfast the night before, spend most of your time wandering around malls looking for the ultimate soft yogurt and muttering: "How come the kids don't call? How come the kids don't call?" The eighties, you'll have a major stroke, and you end up babbling with some Jamaican nurse who your wife can't stand, but who you call mama. Any questions?

Obviously, the students just stare at him, wondering what he's just said. He has successfully unloaded his own despondent feelings but failed to connect with the kids. Sound familiar?

Connecting with our children is sometimes very difficult. Like ocean waves, your ability to communicate with them may come and go. These stages can happen at any time. Several mothers were gathered one evening when the subject of the "worst stage" of childhood came up. "If I can just get through the twos," one mother moaned.

"No, they're a breeze compared with the beginning-of-school stage," came a quick reply.

"And how about those teen years," groaned a third.

Then, during a lull in the conversation, the only grandmother in the group added seriously, "Just wait until they're forty-two!"

LET'S PLAY A GAME

So how do we earn deep influence over our sons and daughters? How do we sustain it over time, even as they become teenagers? How do we get to the place where we can share important words and they actually listen to us?

Probably the best way to answer that question is to play a little game. I want you to answer two personal questions about your past. Think carefully. First, although you may have never had a mentor in your growing up years, can you think of one person you really admired? They had authority in your life. They had influence. It may have been a coach, grandparent, teacher, uncle, or aunt. Try to think of one person.

Now, with this person in mind, isolate one quality about them that gave them such influence in your life. Can you think of a quality? It might have been their acceptance of you. It may have been their integrity or their listening skills or their affirmation. What do you think? Your answer may inform you about what you should do with your child.

Ninety percent of times I have played this mental game with people, they share a quality that has more to do with attitude than aptitude. It was about their heart more than their head. In other words, the "stuff" that earned influence in their life was not high IQ, lots of talent, or money. It was, in fact, qualities of the heart that any of us can acquire if we choose to do so. All of us can build an influential life! We can earn influence if we make the right decisions about how we'll relate to our children.

How to Gain Influence

About ten years ago, I put together a little acronym as I worked with students. It has served to remind me hundreds of times how I can gain influence in the life of a young person. I took the word "INFLUENCE" and used each letter to remind me of what good leaders have done to gain influence in others' lives. If you'll practice these nine elements, I believe you'll increase your influence with your child.

I—Investment in Them.

The greatest mentors I know make deliberate deposits in those they are mentoring. We, too, must choose to invest in our kids. This may mean consistently giving them books, CDs, tapes, or videos to consume. It may be giving them time. It may mean giving them words of praise. We need to keep their "love tank" full. It is our first priority as a parent.

You likely remember hearing about Charles Andrew "Andy" Williams. He is the fifteen-year-old freshman who took a pistol and started spraying Santana High School with bullets, during the 2000–2001 school year. He left two people dead and fourteen others injured. What's sad is how unnecessary this tragedy was. Andy had told a student and an adult that he planned to do this. No one was in touch with how angry he was or how deeply he hurt. Too many withdrawals, not enough deposits.

One teacher said, "When I was in the classroom I saw it happen time and time again. A student would be doing well, and then for no reason there was a change in their personality, their grades dropped, and they became a discipline problem. Each time I was able to find out what was going on, the trail led to problems in the home."[1] Investments in the children had stopped, and it was apparent to all.

Many of those parenting today are baby boomers, those of a generation who rejected the rights of parents to be authority figures in their lives. They insisted that no one over thirty could be trusted. Now, these same baby boomers are parents, and they are realizing with shock the rebellion they chose often comes home to roost. While the millennial generation may be cooperative as a whole, we almost always reap what we sow. My suggestion is this: Invest now, and enjoy the dividends of that investment later. My friends, Ron and Judy Blue, say: "Keep an open door policy with your kids. Let them talk with you about any subject. When they're teens, have food available as their friends visit, and you'll keep them and their friends around. Keep their love tank full."

N—Natural with Them.

I laugh when I see parents try so hard to impress their kids. Kids pick up on how unnatural it is when parents attempt to do something sensational or try to talk kid lingo. CNN reported that the mother of a fifteen-year-old girl allowed a male stripper to appear at her slumber party. CNN said, "Although she claims her daughter hired him without her knowledge, she said she only let him continue his act to avoid embarrassing her daughter."

This poor mother. Reading between the lines, she desperately wanted to be relevant and not be such an old "stick-in-the-mud." Unfortunately, she forfeited something more important. In trying to be a buddy, she relinquished her ability to be who her daughter needed her to be—a mother. The lesson is simple. We are parents. Our job is not to impress our kids but to have a positive impact on them. We need to be ourselves, warts and wrinkles and all. We must show them our humanity, but remain true to our God-given authority.

This may mean we discipline them when they do something wrong but on the same day apologize when we do something wrong. We are not a sage or guru who has all the answers. Nor are we merely a buddy, who has equal authority with them. We don't need to use big words to motivate them. Neither do we need to use "cool" words. We are a parent who must act naturally with them.

My dad has told me many times that his number one challenge as a parent was to be consistent. Consistent in his discipline, example, promises, warnings, follow-through, and love. If he is right about this—that our top challenge is to be consistent as parents—the easiest way to do this is to remain natural.

F—Faith in Them.

Former football player Bill Glass now works with prisoners. He told me some time ago that 80 percent of the inmates in the prisons he visits had parents who told them: "They're going to put you in jail someday."

Everyone needs someone to believe in them. I believe it is one of the best ways to gain influence in a kid's life. We tend to listen to those who believe in us. We like their taste in people! This is why grown men continue to listen to and speak highly of their mothers. I've heard of criminals in the Mafia who still look to their mother for assurance. Why? Mom believes in them. One woman smiled as she said, "No matter how old a mother is, she watches her middle-aged children for signs of improvement."

Deanna was a high school student who worked and studied hard, and usually achieved good grades. She took a course in chemistry, however, that proved to be too tough for her. She applied herself in all the assignments but still flunked the class. This was a first for her, and no doubt it would devastate her family.

Fortunately, her teacher was an unusual man. He took personal interest in Deanna. He believed in her, despite her inability to master chemistry. He did not feel threatened by her failure and knew she would go on to flourish as a college student. However, he still had to give her an "F" on her report card, and this troubled him. He was torn between being honest and expressing his belief in her as a person. He determined to resolve the issue this way. He put an "F" on the report card next to "chemistry" but out on the margin he wrote these words: "We cannot all be chemists— but oh, how we would all love to be Deannas."

What empowering words. Here was a teacher who spoke both grace and truth. There is an art to being honest in our evaluation, yet expressing faith in a child at the same time. I believe it is impossible to really mentor a young person without believing in them.

L—Listening to Them.

Listening is a lost art we must recover. We lose both trust and intimacy when we fail to listen. Let me illustrate. Our worst nightmare is to get an emergency phone call in the middle of the night. One mother got such a call, and it provided a marvelous lesson for her. The phone rang just as her clock radio read midnight. She rubbed her eye as she grabbed the receiver to answer "Hello?" She said later,

My heart pounded, I gripped the phone tighter, and eyed my husband who was now turning to inquire who it was. I panicked as I heard a faint female voice on the line. "Mama?" the voice answered. I could hardly hear the whisper over the static. But my thoughts immediately went to my daughter. When the desperate sound of a crying voice became clear on the line, I grabbed for my husband and squeezed his wrist.

"Mama, I know it's late, but don't . . . don't say anything until I finish. And before you ask, yes, I've been drinking. I nearly ran off the road a few miles back and . . ." She paused. "And I got so scared. All I could think about was how it would hurt you if a policeman came to your door and said I'd been killed. I want . . . to come home. I know running away was wrong. I should have called you days ago but I was afraid." Immediately, I pictured my daughter's face in my mind, and my fogged senses became clear enough to talk: "I think . . ."

"No! Please let me finish! Please!" She pleaded, not so much in anger, but in desperation. I paused and tried to think of what to say. Before I could go on, she continued. "I'm pregnant, Mama. I know I shouldn't be drinking now . . . especially now, but I am scared, Mama."

The voice broke again, and I bit my lip, feeling my own eyes fill with moisture. I looked at my husband, who sat silently mouthing, "Who is it?" I shook my head, and when I didn't answer, he jumped up and returned seconds later with the portable phone to his ear. She must have heard the click in the line, because she asked, "Are you still there? Please don't hang up on me! I need you. I feel so alone."

"Go on," I said. "I won't hang up."

"I should have told you, Mama. But when we talk, you just keep telling me what I should do. You read all those pamphlets on how to talk about sex and all, but all you do is talk. You don't listen to me. You never let me tell you how I feel. It's like my feelings don't exist. Because you're my mother, you think you have all the answers, but sometimes I don't need answers. I just want someone to listen."

I swallowed the lump in my throat and stared at the "how to talk to your kids" pamphlets scattered at my nightstand.

"I could hear you preaching about how I shouldn't drink and drive, so I called a taxi, Mama. I'm comin' home," she finished.

"Please wait for the taxi, honey. Don't hang up until the taxi is there." In minutes, I heard the cab pull up and we said goodbye. Only then did I feel my tension easing. She was safe.

Hanging up the phone, I looked at my husband and said: "We have to learn to listen."

Both of us then walked into our daughter's room, where she lay fast asleep. "Do you think that poor girl will ever know she called a wrong number?" my husband asked.

"Maybe it wasn't such a wrong number after all," I whispered.

Hmmm. Those parents learned a valuable lesson, at someone else's expense. I believe we earn our right to speak by listening. People's favorite voice to hear is their own voice, and when parents listen, they speak volumes about the value of their child. In fact, we motivate faster through listening than through great speeches. Listening is an act of care and intimacy.

U—Understanding of Them.

This one is crucial. We become better mentors for our kids, not when we know more information, but when we know more about them. As I stated earlier, good parents earn the keys to the heart of those young people in whom they invest. They communicate based on their child's bent. For my wife and me, we have to mentor Bethany differently than we do Jonathan. Our daughter is very laid back. Our son is extremely energetic. They require us to parent in different ways. Our discipline is different. Our rewards are different. Our communication is different. Gary Chapman wrote a marvelous book years ago on the *Five Languages of Love*. Every parent should learn the child's primary and secondary language of love. Which language does your child prefer? The five languages are:

1. Quality Time—spending time hanging out with them

2. Words of Affirmation—verbally expressing your approval

3. Deeds of Service—doing something for them out of love

4. Tangible Gifts—giving them something they really want

5. Physical Affection—touching and holding them as a gift

Understanding my family members' languages of love has revolutionized our marriage and has given me a stronger influence in the life of my son and daughter. The other day, my eight-year-old son had a tough day. We sent him to his room for some time out. Later, I went up to his room, and we talked and prayed together. Then, he was quiet, as though he was waiting for me to do something. Finally, I said, "What are you doing?"

"I need you to do what you usually do to make me feel better," he said.

It was then I realized he expected me to speak his language of love. He was waiting for some affirming words and a hug. He knew that I knew what to do.

When we understand the uniqueness of our children, we pour into them in a more relevant fashion. We find ways to communicate and teach that speak to them in a personal way. Wisdom is knowing what to say. Relevance is knowing how to say it.

E—Encouragement to Them.

I shudder to think of the times I miss opportunities to encourage my children. I don't think we can fulfill the role of a leadership mentor unless we master this art. We need it to survive. When kids don't get encouragement, sometimes they'll even ask for it. One dad told me he was out in the backyard with his daughter, preparing to play a little baseball. She told him, "OK, Dad. I'll hit the ball, you say 'Nice job!'"

Years ago, an experiment was conducted to measure people's capacity to endure pain. How long could a bare-footed person stand in a bucket of ice water? It was discovered that when there was someone else present offering encouragement and support, the person standing in the ice water could tolerate the pain twice as long as when there was no one present.

Good mentors find the good in others and affirm it. They magnetically attract others, because people love to be around encouragement. Our goal should be to encourage in a timely and sincere way. Too many syrupy words that aren't backed up with action can have the reverse effect. Don't just say nice things; say them when they count; be specific and sincere. Having worked with college students since 1979, I have seen too many kids who don't even listen to their parents because their words are so fake. Julian Lennon was abandoned by his father, Beatle John Lennon, when he was five years old. Do you think dad's words carry any weight with him? When he was thirty-five, he said in an interview that he thought his dad was fake. He said, "I felt he was a hypocrite. Dad could talk about peace and love out loud to the world, but he could never show it to his wife and son. How can you talk about peace and love and have a family in bits and pieces—no communication, adultery, divorce? You can't do it, not if you're being true and honest with yourself."[2]

N—Navigate for Them.

I have not seen a generation of young people so hungry for direction as the one I see today. Adults have paid so much attention to tolerating all points of view and being politically correct that we're afraid to offer words that guide. Now we live in a world desperate for wise counsel. And while you may feel a parent is the last person a kid is going to listen to, think again. Although the influence of friends increases in their teen years, I am meeting more and more parents who've maintained the strongest voice in their kids' life all through high school and college. Their secret? They practice the components of this little acronym for INFLUENCE. Navigation is an earned right and a learned art.

I saw a cute cartoon that showed two boys walking to school, discussing their parents. One of them said: "I've figured out a system for getting along with my mom. She tells me what to do and I do it." Oh how I wish my kids would discover that same system! Wouldn't it be wonderful to be as brilliant as our children thought we were when they were very young and only half as stupid as they think we are when they're teenagers?

In the early years, being a good navigator means training your kids how to think through choices and problems. You want them to depend on you at first, but then learn how to think things through so that they need you less. This can be quite a challenge, especially when you are the one the family looks to for wisdom. Just ask several million moms across America.

A man was delivering a package from a department store. He knocked at the customer's door and a five-year-old boy answered. "Hello, little fellow," said the delivery man. "Are you here all alone?" "Yes," said the little boy. "Mom's in the hospital, and my brother and my two sisters and my daddy and me are here all alone."

I have one brief footnote on offering navigation to your kids. As they mature, begin providing options for them to choose from. Don't make as many decisions for them. This is part of becoming a leader and part of maturing. Perhaps you could suggest three or four ways of solving a problem, then let them make and own the final decision. Being a good navigator means teaching them how to navigate their own life. They must learn responsibility, decision-making skills, and character if they're to do it well.

C—Concern for Them.

This one is obvious. If we hope to gain influence with our kids (especially as teenagers!), we must display concern, care, and compassion. This ingredient is all about demonstrating love for your child. My wife and I try to communicate in three key ways, visually, verbally, and vulnerably. As I travel, I have noticed when I communicate love to the students I teach and equip, it is almost always reciprocated. Love begets love. They become teachable. As parents, we love unconditionally—with no strings attached—but, when we do love, a tangible by-product is influence.

One mother confirmed this fact. She wrote: "It was Open School Night for my eight-year-old son, and the teacher greeted me with a huge smile. 'Last week I asked the children to name four things essential for survival. I think you'll like your son's answer,' she said, handing me Michael's paper. It read: 'To survive, I need water, air, food, and my mother.'"

Why would an eight-year-old say this? Because he already understood his need for love. Another eight-year-old boy wrote an essay in school entitled, "What a Mom Means to a Kid":

"A mother is a person who takes care of her kids and gets their meals, and if she's not there when you get home from school, you wouldn't know how to get your dinner and you wouldn't feel like eating anyhow."

I know one family who found a creative way to feel each other's love. On a game night, they did a role reversal. Each member became someone else. Not only was it humorous, but it allowed the kids to step into the shoes of their parents and vice versa. For example, a teenager (played by a parent) comes home after curfew and is confronted by a parent (played by a teenager). Or, two parents (played by kids) talk about how they should discipline their child. Or, Mom and Dad (played by two kids) talk to a child (played by an adult) about improving their performance at school or about sex! (This one was hilarious to hear about!)

E—Enthusiasm Over Them.

Kids are attracted to enthusiasm and passion. Good mentors exhibit a zeal and passion for the young person they mentor. It is not merely enthusiasm in general. It is enthusiasm directed at the life of the child. How can anyone not want to follow a person who is passionate about their life, their future, and their interests? This is why grandparents are so popular with grandkids. Those grandparents are excited about anything that has to do with those kids. And the kids know it!

I am not suggesting you try to change your temperament in order to do this. If you are a quiet person, you don't need to artificially conjure up some loud fanaticism; it would not be genuine. I am talking about a keen interest inside of you for your child's growth that comes out in a natural way. I know many parents who have a quiet passion. Some of my favorite mentors are quiet giants. But they are passionate people. If enthusiasm exists inside of a parent, it will find a way to come out. Consider the words of Christ, "Out of the abundance of the heart the mouth speaks" (Matt. 12:34).

What I've found is passion begets passion. Our excitement breeds an excitement in them. Case in point. Shaquille O'Neal is one of the most celebrated players in the NBA. He led the Los Angeles Lakers to a national championship in 2000. When he began, he was the most celebrated rookie in the league. He began with a seven-year contract. There was a lot expected of that twenty-year-old kid. After his first encounter with Patrick Ewing, in which he held his own, a *Sports Illustrated* reporter commented on how calm Shaq was. O'Neal responded, "It takes a lot to get me excited." Then, he added this interesting comment. "You know what gets me excited? When my mom tells me she loves me."[3]

With $40 million committed to him, while riding on the crest of popularity, the thing that gets him excited is his mother's love.

PAYING THE PIPER

Let me ask you a question. What might happen if you practiced these nine ingredients year after year? I believe your influence will only grow. There may be months when you don't feel very influential, but this is how it's done with your kids.

I—Investment in Them.
N—Natural with Them.
F—Faith in Them.
L—Listening to Them.
U—Understanding of Them.
E—Encouragement to Them.
N—Navigate for Them.
C—Concern for Them.
E—Enthusiasm Over Them.

Several decades ago, a movie came out, *Paying the Piper*. It told the story of a father whose influence on his daughter came back to haunt him. He failed to see how much children watch their parents—and reciprocate their behavior. As a teenager, the young lady asks if she can go out on a date. Dad agrees to let her go, but sets a curfew.

Late that night, the father waits and waits for his daughter to return home. She has missed her curfew. Finally, there is a knock at the door. When Dad answers it, he realizes his worst nightmare. It is a police officer, informing him that his daughter has been in an awful accident. She and her date were drinking and swerved into traffic. Both of them died.

The father's grief turns to anger. He becomes determined to find what bar or liquor store sold alcohol to a minor. His daughter was only sixteen. A large part of the film depicts his search to uncover the negligent person who would allow teens to drink. He wants to kill them!

Finally, the movie climaxes as the depressed father sits down on his own easy chair, in defeat. Alas, he has not found the culprit. He is weary. He is despondent. He needs a drink himself. So, he gets up and opens the cabinet where he stores his alcohol—to find it is empty. There is only a note from his daughter, written the night of the car accident: "Dear Daddy. Thanks for letting me go on this date. I took a bottle of your finest. I thought you wouldn't mind, since you like to celebrate with it yourself . . ."

Yes, your kids are watching. And, like it or not, you do influence them more than anyone else in the world.

Reflect and Respond

1. On a scale of 1 to 10, how would you rate your level of influence on your child?

2. Which of the ingredients in the word INFLUENCE do you practice naturally?

3. Where do you need to improve?

15

THE BIG IDEA

*We're so busy giving our kids what we didn't have
that we don't take time to give them what we did have.*
—JOE WHITE

ONE OF THE MOST RIVETING FILMS I'VE SEEN over the last ten years is *Stand and Deliver.* It's the true story of computer technician Jaime Escalante, who gave up a booming career to become a high-school teacher in the barrio of East Los Angeles. His students were underachievers, who couldn't care less about learning. Many of them were gang members. Most of them didn't know their fathers. Escalante willingly took students on that others didn't want to bother with. His subject was calculus, but the class was only a launching pad for his life lessons. He knew he had to do something unusual in order to spark these students. So—he taught them, had them over for dinner, modeled proper approaches to problem solving, and evaluated their attempts, inside and outside his classroom. He transformed teenagers that others had given up on and who had given up on themselves. He took eighteen students who struggled with fractions and long division and took them to honors-level calculus. He challenged them to strive for excellence. And they responded. These chronic underachievers became outstanding students, and many of them became leaders.

How? A committed teacher put himself on the line for his students. He did the unorthodox. He helped them believe in themselves and believe in something beyond themselves. He called out the best in them. He dared to do whatever it took to transform them.

May his tribe increase.

I've lost count of the number of stories I've read about adults, both parents and teachers, who have made a difference in the lives of students. Jaime Escalante is just one of hundreds of such stories. It's interesting to note, in every case there is a common thread. In each instance, the adult did more than merely give a sterile lecture. There was relationship. There was example. There was some unique experience they had together. There was honest evaluation. And before it was over, the child had been revolutionized.

Think of the movies that illustrate this theme, over the last ten to fifteen years: *Stand and Deliver, Dead Poets Society, The Karate Kid, Simon Birch, Music of the Heart, Finding Forrester,* and *Mr. Holland's Opus.* The list goes on and on. These stories move me because I somehow know that transforming a child's life will require me to pay a price. I may have to do the unusual.

This chapter is all about doing the unusual in a systematic way. Often I meet parents who want to mentor their kids but don't know how to do it when they finally get the opportunity to speak into their life. I have good news for you. I believe the answer is simple. It is not easy, but it is simple. Chapter Fourteen was about what you need to do as a parent. This chapter is about what they need to get as a child. I'm going to try and boil down the entire process into four activities. To be honest, these activities are part of any effective training process. Dr. John C. Maxwell compiled a similar list years ago. I have simply modified the list and applied them to parents and mentors.

What's the Big IDEA?

The four activities that spell "IDEA" represent what kids need to become leaders:

> I—INSTRUCTION in a life-related context.
> D—DEMONSTRATION in a life-related context.
> E—EXPERIENCE in a life-related context.
> A—ASSESSMENT in a life-related context.

I am suggesting as your child learns, you can accelerate the process by doing these four activities. They should get to hear about it; see it; participate in it; and evaluate their progress. These four building blocks transform us all. Let's see how this might look at home.

INSTRUCTION . . . IN A LIFE-RELATED CONTEXT

Somewhere in the beginning of any learning process, kids need to hear instruction. Public and private schools have mastered the art of the lecture. And while we may poke fun at the very sound of the term "lecture," it is a negative word for an important part of learning. All children need to be taught. They need instruction that explains how to think and how to view the world. Without it, they may misinterpret what we do and why we do it.

Research shows that unless kids hear adults verbally explain values, they may not gain an accurate perception of what to believe or practice. Both modeling and talking about principles are necessary. Like oars in a rowboat, if you use just one, you may go in circles. Use both and you make progress.

When we offer instruction, it's like giving a compass to our children. They can hear our logic and sense our passion by the tone of our voice. We can teach them how to process information and make sense of their day. It is crucial in the development of their leadership. I believe we have no idea what kind of impression we make as we have these discussions with our kids. In his book, *The Effective Father*, Gordon MacDonald writes about Boswell, the famous biographer of Samuel Johnson. It is said of Boswell that he often referred to a special day in his childhood when his father took him fishing. The day was fixed in his mind, and he often reflected on the many things his father taught him during their day together.

After having heard of that particular excursion so often, it occurred to someone much later to check the journal that Boswell's father kept and determine what had been said about the fishing trip from a parental perspective. Turning to that date, it said: "Gone fishing today with my son. A day wasted."

Do you recognize the value of instructing your child? Can you see how the two of you might create a memory around a simple afternoon of sharing, as you fish, fly a kite, eat an ice-cream cone, or walk through the woods during a weekend camping trip? Are your antennas up to spot what your child needs? Do you see their strengths and can you capitalize on them as you talk about the future? Can you envision their potential as you share with them? Elbert Hubbard said, "There is something that is much more scarce, more rare than ability. It is the ability to recognize ability."[1] Average people have a way of achieving extraordinary things for teachers, leaders, or parents who are patient enough to wait until ability becomes apparent. The history books are full of stories of gifted persons whose talents were overlooked by a procession of people until someone believed in them.

Isaac Newton did poorly in grade school. Einstein was four years old before he could speak and seven before he could read. A newspaper editor fired Walt Disney because he had no good ideas. Leo Tolstoy flunked out of college, and Wernher Von Braun failed ninth-grade algebra. Haydn gave up ever making a musician of Beethoven, who seemed a slow and plodding young man with no apparent talent, except his belief in music."[2]

Comprehending and Connecting Where They Are

Our lesson is clear. People develop at different rates. Everyone has hidden ability. The best parents are on the lookout for hidden capacities in their kids, and teach them accordingly. I mentioned in Chapter Ten that I like to use mealtime for instruction. Our family loves to talk, learn, and laugh at the dinner table. The Council of Economic Affairs did a report on "Teens and Their Parents in the Twenty-first Century." It confirms the power of dinner conversation. It reveals that more than 50 percent of teens who don't eat dinner with their parents have sex by age fifteen or sixteen. By contrast, the number drops 20 percent for teens who do eat dinner with their parents. Teens aged fifteen to sixteen who don't eat dinner regularly are twice as likely to attempt suicide, according to the report.

When we share with our kids in this kind of safe setting, I feel we are giving them a compass for life. It will provide bearings for them as they look for direction in the future. Sometimes it appears to go in one ear and out the other, but I remain hopeful. I know if I am consistent, something has to soak in. It depends on the season they are in.

Ann Landers published a list about how kids view their father at different stages of their life. I chuckled as I related to it, then reflected as I thought about my own kids:

My Father When I Was . . .

Four years old: My daddy can do anything.

Five years old: My daddy knows a whole lot.

Six years old: My dad is smarter than your dad.

Eight years old: My dad doesn't exactly know everything.

Ten years old: In the olden days when my dad grew up, things were different.

Twelve years old: Oh well, Dad doesn't know anything about that. He is too old to remember his childhood.

Fourteen years old: Don't pay any attention to my father. He is so old-fashioned.

Twenty-one years old: Him? My Lord, he's hopelessly out-of-date.

Twenty-five years old: Dad knows a little bit about it, but then he should because he has been around so long.

Thirty years old: Maybe we should ask Dad what he thinks. After all, he's got experience.

Thirty-five years old: I'm not doing a single thing until I talk to Dad.

Forty years old: I wonder how Dad would have handled it. He was so wise and had a world of experience.

Fifty years old: I'd give anything if Dad were here now so I could talk this over with him.

Too bad I didn't appreciate how smart he was. I could have learned a lot.

DEMONSTRATION . . . IN A LIFE-RELATED CONTEXT

Model the principle you want your child to learn. I don't think we can divorce training from modeling. I must set the example and allow my kids to see what they must do before I expect them to do it. Like a blacksmith in old England who would take an apprentice under his wing, we must handle our children as young leadership apprentices. It is show and tell, not merely tell and tell. (Most parents would much rather just tell!)

What's scary is, kids learn faster through seeing, than hearing, whether we like it or not. Our example is a primary training instrument, whether it is good or bad. A picture is worth a thousand words.

Think about your memories of growing up. My guess is you probably remember more things that were done than were said. You likely retained a very limited amount of exact quotes but can vividly remember scenes played out in your memory banks. Why? Listeners more readily remember and believe what a person does than what he or she says. I recognize this as a speaker, standing before audiences each week. I know I must model what I say, off the platform. People do what people see. I can't count the number of times I have heard a young person remind me of something I did, when I didn't realize anyone was watching. Over and over I will think to myself: *They noticed that?*

Andrew Murray, the famous minister from South Africa, had four brothers and three sisters. Each of the eight siblings turned out to be a most outstanding individual. One day his mother was asked how she managed to raise eight of the most marvelous children that had ever graced the state. She said she had only one secret. She tried to live before them exactly the kind of life she wanted them to live.

What kind of lives are we living before our children? I know I have asked this question of you already, but it must be underscored. Are we showing them an example of love, vision, wise decisions, and convictions? Or are we showing them an example of irritability, shortsightedness, and deceitfulness? I heard a father teach his son and two daughters about being honest, over and over. One day, however, I was at their house, when the phone rang. As his son went to answer it, Dad said, "Tell them I'm not here." Hmmm. What are they learning? The child steals a piece of candy and gets a spanking. Then he washes his hands and dries them on a Hilton towel!

Giving a Face to a Principle

From the time our kids were three years old, my wife and I have taught them about reaching out to the poor and underprivileged. We recognized that eventually, talk wouldn't be enough. Our kids would begin to think it's okay just to talk about doing good things—but we don't have to actually do anything. So, in 1999 we sponsored a child in Africa. His name is Franco. We send him money each month. We have his picture up on our refrigerator. We pray for him every night at bedtime. We have sent packages to him. We've received letters from him. We plan to visit Franco one day to meet him face to face. But for now, our kids have a name and a face of a real person who has far less than they do. It is a healthy thing for us, in upper-middle-class America, to experience this.

In addition, our family visits an outreach in Atlanta to feed the homeless. We send gifts at holidays. This last Christmas, we even adopted a project where we bought sheep for children in need in Asia. Our children helped pick them out and used some of their money to get them. The point is simple. Instruction was necessary but it wasn't enough. We needed to model for them.

EXPERIENCE . . . IN A LIFE-RELATED CONTEXT

Once we've given our children instruction on a principle and shown them an example of how it looks in real life, we must let them try it out themselves. Nothing galvanizes learning more than experience. We can talk theories until the cows come home, but theory doesn't help anyone unless there is a practical application to it all. I remember reading a Peanuts cartoon in which Lucy interrupted Schroeder, the piano-loving intellectual. She was infatuated with him and desperately wanted to catch his attention. So Lucy hinted at her interest by asking him, "Schroeder, do you know what love is?" Schroeder abruptly stopped his playing, stood to his feet, and said precisely, "Love: noun; to be fond of; to have a strong affection for or an attachment to a person or persons." Then, he sat back down and resumed playing his piano. Lucy sat there stunned and then murmured sarcastically, "On paper, he's great."

Unfortunately, that describes much of our parental training today. On paper, we're great. What we need to do is translate our wonderful principles into real-life experiences for our kids. Like the Dohertys did. Megan Doherty was sixteen when she heard a speech by the executive director of "Camps for Children of Chernobyl." The speech was about how families could sponsor a child and bring them to the U.S. for medical treatment. Her parents had been developing a servant's heart in her, through discussions at home, and this seemed to be a natural place to practice what they preached. Megan and her parents decided to host a child from Chernobyl, but it turned out to be more than they could afford, all told. Megan made presentations to civic organizations and church groups, solicited donations through newspaper articles, flyers, and phone calls, and organized a variety of fund-raising projects. Megan went well beyond her goal.

By 1999, Megan had raised more than $56,000 to bring twenty-nine cancer victims of the 1986 Chernobyl disaster to her town for life-saving medical treatment and dental care that weren't available to them in the Ukraine. This not only changed the life of those young cancer victims; it changed Megan and her family as well. For the rest of this story, see the Prudential Community Awards Web site.

Ron Blue has written a number of books on how to handle personal finances. He and his wife, Judy, wrote a book together on helping children manage money as well. They told me over lunch recently that the best way to build responsible adults is to give them responsibility as kids. Ron and Judy did this very well as parents of five children. Ron believes money is a tool for parents to teach responsibility—but you have to allow them the freedom to take it and fail. He and his wife would give their kids significant amounts of money to spend, to invest, and to give away. They taught them to file it away in envelopes. They even taught them to buy their own clothes and supplies for school. If the kids misspent it, they learned valuable lessons, and never made that mistake again! Ron said he also believes money is a test, to reveal how mature your children are. It helps you evaluate the direction they are moving. Finally, he said it's also a testimony. It speaks of where their heart is and how their character is growing. Once again, however, real-life experience is essential.

Why Is Experience Necessary?

Recently I asked myself the question: Why is it our kids require experience in order to learn? Why can't we just tell them what they need to know and end it there? Why are words not enough? In a conversation with a friend, I got my answer. Dan told me: "As a high schooler, I tried to play guitar. But I was an amateur—I'd learn only a chord a month. At that rate, I figured I'd be seventy-two years old before I could play in a band.

"Then one day a leader in a band I had dreamed of playing in asked me to join. I said yes in a heartbeat. Then he told me that we'd have tons of summer gigs, and that I had two months to learn thirty songs—the lyrics, the chords, everything.

"I was not deterred. I ate those songs up. I breathed those songs. I practiced till my fingers bled, because I wanted to do it so badly. That was my secret. I learned so much in those two months because I was using what I learned."

This is how our human mind is wired. We learn what we use. Did you ever take a foreign language in school? I bet you forgot most of it, unless you kept using it. This is why experience is so crucial. When it comes to any subject, we must use it or we lose it.

Assessment . . . in a Life-Related Context

It is good to instruct our kids, but it is even better to *model it for them* as well. It is further improvement to let them gain a genuine experience themselves. But experience alone is not the best teacher. Kids can have a bad experience and learn the wrong things. Experience plus evaluation is the best teacher. This is why we cannot afford to neglect careful reflection and assessment at the end of every learning experience.

Albert Mehrabian, a professor at UCLA, says that within thirty days, people forget 90 percent of what they have learned unless it is repeatedly reinforced. In other words, principles must be taught, experienced, and reflected upon over and over. We must debrief what we've learned and practiced together. Practice doesn't make perfect. (Especially if we practice what is wrong!) Practice plus evaluation makes perfect.

Our daughter, Bethany, has entered the baby-sitting stage. She is a young teenager with a maternal instinct. She loves kids. However, she has also entered the phase where she loves to go out with her friends. Last Friday, a group of her friends were planning a group date, and a guy asked her to join in. This is where things got a bit tense. Bethany had agreed to baby-sit for a neighbor on Friday but had not determined what time she was needed. Now she was uncertain whether she could both baby-sit on Friday and go on the group date as well. Tears were shed as she pondered having to say no to either opportunity.

My wife, Pam, and I had to sit down with her and sort things out. After two phone calls, we discovered she couldn't keep both commitments. Bethany didn't want to have to confront the issue and say no to either. Pam and I knew she would have to, and we wanted her to do what was right—which meant keeping her original commitment.

When all was said and done, the three of us sat down and debriefed the situation. We evaluated what we all had learned from it. We made a list of six observations. One was that Bethany doesn't want to baby-sit on Friday nights, at least for now. Another was, we must keep our commitments regardless of better opportunities that come up later. A third was we must do our homework before we make decisions. As I reflect on the weekend, it was a positive experience for all of us (parents, too!) because it gave us a chance to assess our lives and evaluate what we were learning.

John and Camie Fetz are good friends of mine. Recently, they told me one major principle they've tried to instill in their kids—respect. First, respect for authority. Second, respect for others in general, regardless of whether you agree with them. And third, earning the respect of others by living a life worthy of it. This is crucial for leaders to learn.

Their son Ryan just finished a term as junior class co-president. He and a fellow student oversaw the junior-senior prom and banquet at their high school. Planning for this event took the better part of a year, and there were rough spots along the way. Working with different personalities proved to be a challenge. Fortunately, it gave John and Camie a marvelous opportunity to debrief and evaluate how Ryan was living out the principle of respect. All through the year, they had a "leadership project," which served as a laboratory in which Ryan could assess his growth with Mom and Dad. They not only eat dinner together at night but breakfast every weekday morning at 6:00 A.M.! Most of the time, they spend sharing with each other and helping them process what's going on in their lives.

Camie told me their goal is to create an environment where it is safe for the kids to talk about absolutely anything.

EVALUATING LEADERSHIP ABILITY

When parents take this job of assessment seriously, we enter a whole new level of training with our children. We will become more sensitive with our input; we will become more specific with our words; and we will become more specialized with our mentoring times. In short, our training will be even more relevant.

In my attempt to assess the leadership ability of my two children, I have come up with six steps I try to walk them through. This is the process I believe points us in the right direction:

1. Expand Their Horizons.

First, we must broaden their understanding of leadership. Being a leader doesn't mean they have to look like some stereotype they know. Various situations call for various types of leadership. They might fail miserably in one context but succeed in another. Help your child get out of the box and discover that leadership is bigger than any one style and is just as unique as they are.

2. Explore the Possibilities.

Next, we need to help them see what opportunities lie in front of them that they could explore and discover if it fits them. They need to identify their leadership style and where is a most suitable place to serve. You need to give them a big picture view on what's available out in the world.

3. Experiment with Options.

Third, they need to get their feet wet, to step out to experiment with some options that lay in front of them. Help them pursue some possibilities where they can spread their wings and try out this leadership thing. They will never know some things without jumping in and trying them on for size. As I've said, they must get beyond theory.

4. Exercise Their Discernment.

Not all leadership roles will fit who they are, and not all projects will match the scope of responsibility they're ready for. This is where you can be a big help. In this step, help them discern their level of fulfillment. Did they truly enjoy leading on those particular situations? Did they get a sense that this is what they were built to do?

5. Expect Confirmation.

Our children need to listen to others around them who know them well. What do their mature friends say about them? Does anyone confirm that they are gifted and suited for a particular task? Do they receive encouragement from more than Mom and Dad to continue to try another opportunity? Do others sense they are cut out to lead there?

6. Examine the Results.

Finally, they must learn to look at what kind of fruit they've borne in their leadership roles. The proof will always be in the pudding. Did they accomplish the goal? Were people used as a team? Did they share the power and the responsibility with others? Did they exceed expectations? These are the kinds of questions true leaders always ask and answer with a resounding yes!

THE POWER OF ONE

I need to say something again. I realize that some of these steps are only appropriate for kids as they enter their teens and beyond. Don't feel awkward if you think your son or daughter is unready for some of them. Remember, kids all develop at different rates. One thing is sure, however. Regardless of how slowly they mature, "the power of one" always stands.

This last year, I was impressed with the advertisement the U.S. Army has chosen to use on TV. They end their commercials calling recruits to become "an army of one." In other words, although they will serve in a platoon or battalion, they are to go out fully equipped, because one person can make all the difference in the world.

We learned this in the presidential election of 2000. President Bush edged out Al Gore because a few individuals chose to vote who could have easily stayed home. It was the power of the individual. The influence of one vote. But it wasn't the first time we learned this lesson. Oliver Cromwell won control of England by one vote in 1645. During the American Revolution, anti-British sentiment was huge. A bill was presented to the Continental Congress that would have replaced the English language in America in favor of German. It was defeated by one vote. In 1845, the Senate voted to admit Texas to the union by one vote. Senator Hannigan changed his mind at the last minute and voted in favor of its admission. Ironically, the senator himself had won his election to office by only one vote.

On November 8, 1923, the leaders of the tiny Nazi party met in a Munich tavern and elected Adolf Hitler as their leader—by a margin of one vote. What disastrous world war might have been avoided if that one person had voted differently.

These are only reminders again of the influence one person can have and the difference one person can make. This is why we are taking pains to nurture the leader in our children. Who knows what your child might do. An army of deer led by a lion is more to be feared than an army of lions led by a deer.

Reflect and Respond

1. Choose one leadership principle. How could you practice the big IDEA to teach it?

2. What modeling are you doing to allow your kids to see what a leader looks like?

3. How do you know when your child has really learned a leadership truth?

16

THE MENTOR'S EQUATION

*The most important thing that parents can teach
their children is how to get along without them.*
—FRANK A. CLARK

UNITED STATES HISTORY IS FULL OF INTRIGUING stories. Some of the most interesting ones surround the men who've served as president of our nation. One such story involves a president you may not know.

President-elect Zachary Taylor was scheduled to take office on Sunday, March 4, at noon. Being a deeply committed Christian, he refused to be inaugurated on his day of worship. Taylor announced he would be inaugurated on Monday at noon, instead. However, the Constitution forbade President Polk to serve one more day of office. This left Congress with an interesting dilemma. The U.S. was going to experience one full day without a publicly elected president. The Senate had no alternative than to appoint a man to serve for twenty-four hours, from noon Sunday to noon Monday. The senators chose David Rice Atchison, the head of the Senate.

However, the last week of the Polk administration was so hectic for Senator Atchison that he retired late Saturday evening after instructing his landlady not to awaken him for any reason. She followed his orders. Atchison slept through Sunday morning, Sunday afternoon, all through

Sunday night, Monday morning—and finally awoke at 2:00 P.M. on Monday afternoon. He slept through his entire term of office!

Wow. Atchison was president for a day and never took advantage of it. This may sound trite, but sometimes I feel like David Rice Atchison. As a parent, I'm so tired from the day-to-day grind, I often miss golden windows of opportunity to make a difference in my children's lives. I get caught "slumbering" emotionally. Later, I look back and see I was oblivious to the chance I had to mentor them. Hindsight is always 20/20. Someone once said, "The trouble with being a parent is that by the time you're experienced, you're unemployed."

SEIZING THE OPPORTUNITY

In this final chapter, I want to encourage you. I'm going to finish by providing a simple equation based on an interview I had with a gentleman two months before finishing this book. I believe the most memorable and the most practiced principles are the simplest ones, and I hope you will find this chapter very simple and very memorable.

I have attempted to lay out ideas, principles, stories, and steps for you to use as you nurture the leader in your children. I recognize you might just be overwhelmed by this task, especially with all the information I've thrown at you! Let me now attempt to boil it down to a simple equation that anyone can use. I'm challenging you to take the initiative. Whatever you do with this book, please accept my challenge to make mentoring a priority. This equation will work if you take your job of developing your child's potential seriously. Rabbi Kassel Abelson reminds us: "The Hebrew word for parents is *horim*, and it comes from the same root as *moreh*, the word for teacher. The parent is, and remains, the first and most important teacher that the child will ever have."

David Wilkerson wrote, "Good parents do not always produce good children, but devoted, dedicated, hard working mothers and fathers can weigh the balance in favor of decency and the building of moral character. Every word and deed of a parent is a fiber woven into the character of a child, which ultimately determines how that child fits into the fabric of society."[1]

THE MENTOR'S EQUATION

Here is the equation I promised. It spells out what kids need in order to be transformed:

$$\text{IMITATION} + \text{INTERVIEW} = \text{IMPACT}$$

By imitation, I mean kids need an example to imitate. If we're going to foster leadership, they need us to show them what it looks like. By interview, I mean kids need a chance to talk with the person who's offering the example and process what they've seen. They need to interpret leadership behaviors. These are fundamentals that make them want to try it themselves. When we provide a model to imitate for our kids, coupled with an interview of that person to explain why they do what they do, it results in major impact. As I have stated before, kids need to see leadership demonstrated. Then, they need to process and interpret what they saw, in some sort of interview. Put another way, DEMONSTRATION plus CONVERSATION equals TRANSFORMATION.

AN INTERVIEW WITH BEN

I had the undeserved privilege of interviewing a father who practiced this equation with his son. We had a marvelous time, sharing what it means to help our kids grow up and become men and women others want to follow.

His name is Ben Ferrell. His son's name is Parker. All through Parker's life, his dad has focused on developing him into a godly man of character. Like most dads, Ben's felt inadequate for the task, but he determined to find a way to give Parker all the tools he needed for manhood, even if he had to get help doing it. As his son grew older, Ben began to see his strengths and weaknesses, and sought for a way to mentor and invest in him more completely. He realized that he may not have all the resources to help Parker achieve his goals. He began to pray and put his "antennas" up to find how to coach Parker so that he could reach his potential.

When Parker turned twelve, Ben got an idea. The two sat down and made a list of eight men whom both of them respected—eight influential men whose lives reflected the kind of life Parker desired for himself. It was a mutual decision for them on who those men might be. When they arrived at their choices, Ben sat down and wrote letters to each one of them. He requested a huge favor. He asked them if they would be willing to spend one day that next year, between Parker's twelfth and thirteenth birthdays, with his son. He asked them to spend that day letting Parker watch them, talk to them, even work with them if that's what they chose to do on that day. Parker would shadow these men, one on one, for one full day. Ben said, "If you choose to do a special event with Parker, that's fine. If you choose to have him work all day with you, that's fine, too. But whatever you do," he continued, "I'd like you to share one 'life-message' with him. Take some time and speak to him about an issue you feel is foundational to life. If you like, you can even choose to do something that day with Parker that communicates your 'life-message.' Just find a way to work in your life theme. I trust you and welcome your input in my son's life."

Needless to say, each one of the men was more than happy to do this. They welcomed the chance to speak into the life of a young, emerging leader like Parker. All through the year, these one-day appointments took place. Some men took Parker out to work. One man was a farmer, and he and Parker worked side by side all day on the farm. Another man took him fishing and talked to him about the importance of prayer and solitude. All eight of them were different. Some focused on helping him discover his gifts and strengths, others on his integrity and character. One man spoke to him about his future and how his values would shape his decisions down the road. It was a life-changing day for both Parker and the eight men who spent their day with him.

On his thirteenth birthday, a big barbecue was planned for Parker. Ben invited all eight men to attend and to celebrate. They laughed as they reflected on their time together and shared stories of how they remembered it, all while enjoying grilled chicken or beef out in the back yard. The food and presence of all eight men alone made it a memorable night.

Afterward, however, the main event took place. On the counsel of Dad, Parker had written a personal thank-you note to each of the men who had invested in his life that year. He read each letter aloud in the presence of the others. The thirteen-year-old shared with them how significant his time was with them. He talked about what he'd learned from them and what it meant to watch them for a full day. He singled out the life message they had shared with him and what each message meant to him and how he planned to implement it in his life. Thanks to Dad, he had taken notes through the year and was prepared for this night.

Next, each man was permitted to respond to Parker. This was their chance to share in the presence of the others what they saw in Parker as a young man. They responded to his grateful letter but didn't stop there. Each one spoke of his potential. Some challenged him to flee the temptations that his peers would fall into. The gentleman who took Parker out on his farm affirmed Parker's work ethic, saying he was the hardest worker he'd seen on his farm. Several spoke into his life about his future, and what they envisioned Parker could do if he set his mind and heart to do it. All of them generously lavished him with love and strength and affirmation. There was not a dry eye in the room that night.

Each man talked about how the experience rekindled a fire in their own heart, to be a man of character and vision; to be a man of God. The evening closed when Ben asked all the men to gather around his son and pray for him. It was a moving prayer time, where they invited God to watch over young Parker, and raise him up to be the man he was created to be.

It was a night to remember. Ben told me later that it actually served as a rite of passage into manhood for Parker. Each of the men committed themselves to be available to Parker as mentors, if he so wished in the future. Down the road, Parker can approach them for advice, to ask questions or to bounce ideas off of them. They also got permission to hold young Parker accountable to pursue his gifts and reach his potential. They became extended family-mentors from the community.

After Parker's thirteenth birthday, he and his dad took a trip together to process what he was thinking and how he was growing. The two of them now plan to put a group together of six to eight pairs of fathers and sons, who will meet every month to affirm and challenge their sons, and offer them direction. Ben and his wife have a younger daughter. Needless to say, plans are under way for her to meet with eight women who will mentor her in a similar way.

After my conversation with Ben, I was ready to burst. I immediately called my wife, Pam, and told her about Ben and Parker, the eight men, and this simple equation. We've decided we want to do something like this for our kids. I know Pam and I don't have all it takes to develop my kids into leaders—we need the help of others whom we trust. So, we've made our lists . . . and we're on our way. With a team of others, we might just get the job done.

THE CLOTHES I GOTTA WEAR

Wherever I go, whatever I do, my wife is always checking to make sure I'm dressed appropriately. If I am about to walk on a platform to speak to an audience, I need to be dressed slightly more formally than they are. If I am going to work around the house, she insists I take off anything nice and wear old work clothes. I am the king of spills and splatters. So—off I go to change out of my formal wear and into my informal wear.

Since mentoring my children in leadership is such a monumental task, I've gotta wear the right clothes for this job, too. I read the scriptures recently, where Paul encourages his readers to "clothe themselves with love" and to "clothe themselves with Christ" (Col. 3:14; Gal. 3:27). This means I must put love on, so it can be seen in my behavior. Love must be my outer garment as well as the centerpiece of my heart. My mom used to talk to me, as a kid, about "wearing a smile" on my face, or "putting on good manners" when I was in public. Again, these have to do with behavioral clothing—the stuff that others see.

I started thinking: What should I wear to nurture and coach my children? What kind of clothes does a mentor own? This is what I came up with. These are the clothes of a mentor.

1. I Must Wear the Pants in the Relationship.

This means I must take initiative and responsibility. I must make the first move and assume responsibility for resourcing them. Leadership is caught more than taught. It begins with being a person your son or daughter will follow. I am the host of the relationship.

2. I Must Give Them the Shirt Off My Back.

This means I must be generous and serve them. I don't know any good mentors who don't possess a servant's heart and a generous spirit.

Control and manipulation will never get the permanent results you are after in your kids. Servant leadership is what wins followship.

3. I Must Throw My Cap Over the Wall.

This means I must demonstrate commitment and vulnerability. Do you remember the story I told about John Kennedy as a boy? He played a game called "Throw your cap over the wall." It taught him to try something that required him to take risks and keep his commitments.

4. I Must Try on Their Glasses.

This means I must see their perspective and identify with their needs and concerns. I must look through the lens of a kid and communicate from where they live. I must respect them if I expect them to know what respect looks like. I must start where their interests lie.

5. I Must Wear Shoes I Want Filled.

This means I must set the example. I must display integrity and model the life I want them to live as adults. I should not be ashamed of my habits and actually welcome them to emulate me. I must recognize my kids will follow my footsteps easier than they follow my advice.

How about you? Are you wearing the right clothes for the job that's in front of you? Are you in uniform and ready for the task to begin? You've just waded through a truck load of material. What are you going to do to nurture the leadership gifts inside your kids? When will you start?

For the last two years, my son, Jonathan, has been in the stage where he loves to try on my shirts, my ties, my belts, and especially my shoes. Oh, how he loves my shoes. Since he's only in the second grade, he thinks they're huge. "I will never fit into these big things," he told me.

I responded by telling him that his doctor predicts he will grow taller than I am and weigh more than I weigh. "You'll fill shoes bigger than those," I concluded. His eyes got large. He smiled as he thought about it. Then, he said: "I'm going to be bigger than my dad!"

That's my hope, son. That's my hope.

About the Author

Dr. Tim Elmore is best known for his leadership among pastors, business leaders, and university students. He is a gifted communicator, author, and illustrator and serves as vice president of EQUIP. EQUIP is a nonprofit organization founded by John C. Maxwell that offers leadership resources and training to three arenas: the academic, urban, and international communities.

Dr. Elmore's work has taken him to twenty-six nations and numerous college and university campuses, and he has worked with international companies and organizations, including Chick-fil-A, Gold Kist, and Habitat for Humanity. Tim and his wife, Pam, reside in Atlanta, Georgia, with their two children.

To contact Tim Elmore or EQUIP ministries for speaking events or student leadership resources, find the Web page at:

www.growingleaders.com. Or, call the toll free number: (888) 993-7847.

NOTES

Chapter One

1. Quoted in *Millennials Rising*, by Neil Howe and William Strauss (New York: Vintage Books 2000), 18.

Chapter Two

1. Jeremiah Creedon, "God with a Million Faces," *Utne Reader*, July/August 1998, no. 88, 42–48.
2. James Gilmore and Joseph Pine, *Work Is Theatre and Every Business a Stage* (Boston: Harvard Business School Press, 1999).
3. Howe and Strauss, *Millennials Rising*, 66.
4. Ibid., 19.
5. Ibid., 26.
6. Dennis Cone, ed., *Current Thoughts and Trends*, October 1998, 11.
7. Ibid.

Chapter Three

1. Howe and Strauss, *Millennials Rising*, 24.
2. Ibid.

Chapter Four

1. Andrew Goldstein, "Paging All Parents," *Time*, 3 July 2000, 47.
2. Rick and Kathy Hicks, *Boomers, Xers and Other Strangers* (Wheaton, IL: Tyndale House, 1999), 328.
3. Ibid., 26.

Chapter Five

1. Sharon Begley, "A World of Their Own," *Newsweek*, 8 May 2000, 56.
2. William Bennett, *The Book of Virtues* (New York: Simon & Schuster, 1993).
3. Thomas Harvey, "The Truth May Soon Be More of a Stranger Than Fiction," *Mission America*, summer 1998, 5–6
4. Norman V. Peale, *Imaging* (New York: Guideposts, 1982), 85.
5. Bridget Hopkinson and Miranda Smith, eds., *Children's History of the 20th Century* (New York: DK Publishing, 1999).

Chapter Six

1. Alexander and Helen Astin, *Leadership Reconsidered: A Kellogg Report* (The W. K. Kellogg Foundation, 2000).
2. Ibid.

Chapter Seven

1. Quoted in www.prudential.com/community/spirit/awards.

Chapter Eight

1. Quoted in www.prudential.com/community/spirit/awards.
2. Ibid.

Chapter Nine

1. *Group Magazine*, November/December 1998, 15, as quoted in *Current Thoughts and Trends*, Discipleship Journal (Colorado Springs, CO), February 1999.
2. John Maxwell, sermon entitled "Characteristics of a Godly Mother," 10 May 1987.
3. *Time*, 23 Nov. 1998, vol. 152, no. 21, 86.

Chapter Ten

1. Parenting Today's Teen, Web site, quoted 16 January 2001.
2. Howe and Strauss, *Millennials Rising*, 236.
3. Jack Canfield et al., *Chicken Soup for the Preteen Soul* (Deerfield Beach, FL: Health Communications, Inc., 2000), 254–55.
4. Ibid 221-24

Chapter Eleven

1. Wayne Muller, quoted in *Credenda Agenda*, 2000, vol. 12, no. 2, 3.
2. Jack Canfield et al., *A Fourth Course of Chicken Soup for the Soul* (Deerfield Beach, FL: Health Communications, Inc., 1995), 136.
3. Gary Smalley and John Trent, *The Blessing* (New York: Pocket Books, 1986).

Chapter Twelve

1. *The London Times*, 23 May 2001, 2–3.
2. Jeffrey Kluger and Alice Park, "So You Want to Raise a Super Kid," *Time*, April 2001, vol. 157, no. 17, 53.

3. Ibid.

4. Jack Canfield, 136.

5. Smalley and Trent, *The Blessing.*

6. Jay McGraw, *Life Strategies for Teens* (New York, NY: Simon and Schuster, 2000).

Chapter Thirteen

1. John Maxwell, *Breakthrough Parenting* (Colorado Springs, CO: Focus on the Family, 1995).

2. David Thomas, *Marriage and Family Living*

Chapter Fourteen

1. Matt Bai, "Anatomy of a Massacre," *Newsweek*, 3 May 1999, 22–31.

2. Julian Lennon, as quoted in *Current Thoughts and Trends* (Colorado Springs, CO: NavPress, 1998), 61.

3. Shaquille O'Neal, as quoted in *Sports Illustrated*, November 1992, 25.

Chapter Fifteen

1. Alan Loy McGinnis, *Bringing Out the Best in People* (Minneapolis, MN: Augsburg Press, 1985).

2. Ibid.

Chapter Sixteen

1. Joe White, *What Kids Wish Parents Knew About Parenting* (West Monroe, LA: Howard Publishing, 1998), 57.

ACKNOWLEDGMENTS

ANYONE WHO WRITES A BOOK RECOGNIZES that it could not have been done without the work of many others. Complementary-gifted people surround me, and I am grateful for their contribution to this manuscript. Let me underscore this team of people.

Dr. John C. Maxwell has empowered me since I joined his staff in 1983. It was he who opened the door for me to write this book. He has been a leadership mentor for me since I was twenty-three years old. Thanks, John, for believing in me.

Sharon Hull faithfully worked next to me—gathering material, reading, filing, and critiquing what you have read. Sharon, you are a godsend. It is a privilege to know you and to work alongside you. Thanks for complementing me.

Reggie Joiner is a creative genius. He is a friend and the inspiration for taking the job of mentoring kids so seriously. As the founder of "FamilyWise," he fed ideas to me, which you have benefitted from here. Thanks, Reggie, for your gifts.

Tracey Fries assisted me in clearing my calendar of any "fat" so I could get away and write. She is the greatest executive assistant I have ever worked with. Thanks, Tracey, for adding so much value to my life.

Holly Moore took the initiative to find out what days I would be writing, and she set those days aside to pray for me. She became my chief prayer warrior. Thanks, Holly, for the tangible and intangible support you consistently offer me. You are a true friend.

Victor Oliver is my publisher. I would not have dared to attempt this project without his input. The book was his idea. Victor—you are brilliant. Thanks for all the breakfasts and red ink on my manuscript. You've become a mentor.

My mom and dad have more to do with this book than anyone will ever know. They have been marvelous parents as they built character and values in me. They modeled what any kid would want in a mentor. I love you, Mom and Dad.

Finally, I must acknowledge my wife and girlfriend, Pam. She thinks I can do anything. (Pssst. Please don't tell her the truth!) Thank you, babe, for believing in me and supporting me so well with your time and effort. Thanks also for joining me as we nurture the leader inside of our own two children. I love you.

—Tim Elmore